W9-BJN-368

POCKET

AMSTERDAM

TOP EXPERIENCES · LOCAL LIFE

CATHERINE LE NEVEZ,
KATE MORGAN, BARBARA WOOLSEY

Contents

Plan Your Trip   4

Clogs on display at a market
RICHARD NEBESKY/LONELY PLANET ©

Explore Amsterdam 33

COVID-19

We have re-checked every business in this book to ensure that it is still open after the COVID-19 outbreak. However, the economic and social impacts of COVID-19 will continue to be felt long after the outbreak has been contained, and many businesses, services and events referenced in this guide may experience ongoing restrictions. Some businesses may be temporarily closed, have changed their opening hours and services, or require bookings; some unfortunately could have closed permanently. We suggest you check with venues before visiting for the latest information.

Special Features

Survival Guide 173

Amsterdam's Top Experiences

Admire art at Rijksmuseum (p102)

IRISPHOTO1/SHUTTERSTOCK ©

Discover the work of a master at the Van Gogh Museum (p106)

Remember the past at Anne Frank Huis (p60)

ANNE FRANK HUIS
PRINSENGRACHT
1

Explore Rembrandt's former home at Museum het Rembrandthuis (p148)

Step into a story book at Begijnhof (p38)

Wander through Vondelpark (p110)

WILL SALTER/LONELY PLANET ©

TRAVELLERPIX/SHUTTERSTOCK ©

Marvel at the opulence of the Royal Palace (Koninklijk Paleis; p36)

Examine ethnographic artefacts at Tropenmuseum (p136)

Dining Out

Amsterdam's sizzling-hot foodie scene boasts a vast array of eating options, such as classic Dutch snacks; reinvented traditional recipes; on-trend establishments pioneering world-first concepts; a wave of new, ultra-healthy eateries, often vegetarian or vegan; and an increasing focus on wine, cocktail and craft-beer pairings.

Dutch Cuisine

Traditional Dutch cuisine revolves around meat, potatoes and vegetables. Typical dishes include *stamppot* (mashed pot) – potatoes mashed with another vegetable (usually kale or endive) and served with smoked sausage and strips of bacon.

Fresh winds are blowing through the Dutch traditional kitchen, breathing new life into centuries-old recipes by giving them a contemporary twist.

Current Trends

Concept restaurants, such as an all-avocado restaurant, are popping up all over the city. Other current trends include gourmet street food (poké bowls, ramen, tacos...) as well as all-day brunch. Foodhallen (p119), in the De Hallen tram depot-turned-cultural complex, has a host of eateries under one roof, and is a fantastic place to take the city's dining temperature.

Best Traditional Dutch

Bistro Bij Ons Honest-to-goodness Dutch classics. (p70)

Pantry A *gezellig* (cosy, convivial) atmosphere and classic Dutch fare. (p92)

Van Dobben Meaty goodness diner-style. (p91)

Best Contemporary Dutch

Gebr Hartering In a seductive canal-side location, the menu changes daily, but is unfailingly delicious. (p158)

Greetje Contemporary Dutch cooking rooted in forgotten Dutch recipes. (p158)

STUDIOPORTOSABBIA/SHUTTERSTOCK ©

De Silveren Spiegel
Refined Dutch cuisine in a romantic step-gabled townhouse. (p48)

Graham's Kitchen Ingredients at this local secret are sourced from the Amsterdam area. (p126)

Best Vegan

Bonboon Elevated vegan cuisine and a terrace overlooking the water. (p160)

Alchemist Garden Vegan heaven, serving delicious gluten- and lactose-free dishes. (p115)

Mr & Mrs Watson Vegan comfort food including a vegan fondue. (p142)

Vegan Junk Food Bar
Plant-based burgers, Dutch *bitterballen* (croquettes; pictured) and more. (p91)

Best Budget

Vleminckx To slather your golden potatoes in mayonnaise, curry or one of the myriad other sauces? (p47)

Braai BBQ Bar Street-food-style hotspot barbecuing tangy ribs. (p115)

Gartine Slow Food sandwiches and a dazzling high tea hide in the Medieval Centre. (p47)

Best Bakeries

Patisserie Holtkamp You're in good company, as the gilded royal coat of arms outside attests. (p85)

Baking Lab A communal oven, baking classes and heavenly breads. (p143)

Dining Out: Top Tips

• Book ahead at places in the middle and upper price brackets. Nearly everyone speaks English. Many places offer online booking options.

• Many restaurants don't accept credit cards. Or if they do, there's often a 5% surcharge. Conversely, an increasing number of places accept cards only. Check first.

Bar Open

Amsterdam is one of the world's wildest nightlife cities. Beyond the Red Light District, Leidseplein and Rembrandtplein, the clubbing scene has expanded thanks to 24-hour-licensed venues. Yet you can easily avoid the hardcore party scene: Amsterdam remains a café (pub) society where the pursuit of pleasure focuses on cosiness and charm.

Cafés

Amsterdam is famed for its historic *bruin cafés* (brown cafes; traditional Dutch pubs). The name comes from the nicotine stains from centuries of use (although recent aspirants slap on brown paint to catch up). Most importantly, the city's brown cafes provide an atmosphere conducive to conversation – and the nirvana of *gezelligheid* (conviviality, cosiness).

Clubbing

Amsterdam is banging on Berlin's door to claim the mantle of Europe's clubbing capital. The electronic music extravaganza **Amsterdam Dance Event** (ADE; www.amsterdam-dance-event.nl; ⏰mid-Oct) is a fixture on the city's calendar, and from 2012 Amsterdam has appointed a *nachtburgemeester* (night mayor), representing and encouraging the city's nightlife and economy (the first city in the world to do so).

Inner-city clubs are integrating into the social fabric, and epic venues (including some with 24-hour licences) are occupying repurposed buildings outside the city centre (accessible by public transport) to avoid noise. In addition to club nights, they mount multi-genre art exhibitions, markets and other diverse cultural offerings.

Best Brown Cafes

In 't Aepjen Candles burn all day long in the time-warped, 500-year-old house. (p49)

Hoppe An icon of drinking history beloved by journalists, bums and raconteurs. (p51; pictured)

De Sluyswacht Swig in the lock-keeper's quarters

across from Rembrandt's house. (p161)

Best Breweries

Brouwerij 't IJ Wonderful independent brewery at the foot of the De Gooyer windmill. (p162)

Brouwerij Troost Sip frothy house-made suds. (p129)

Brouwerij De Prael Socially minded brewery that makes strong organic beers. (p51)

Oedipus Brewery & Tap Room Brilliant brewery in Amsterdam Noord. (p170)

Best Cocktail Bars

Rosalia's Menagerie Dutch heritage–themed cocktails in vintage surrounds. (p160)

Tales & Spirits House infusions and vintage glasses. (p50)

Canvas Edgy, artsy bar with great views atop the former Volkskrant newspaper building, now a flash hotel. (p143)

Door 74 Speakeasy-style bar mixing some of Amsterdam's wildest cocktails. (p94)

Best Coffee

Lot Sixty One Red-hot Amsterdam roastery. (p117)

Scandinavian Embassy Coffee sourced from Scandinavian micro-roasteries. (p128)

Bar Open: Top Tips

○ *Café* means pub; a coffeeshop is where one gets marijuana.

○ *Een bier*, *een pils* or *een vaasje* is a normal-sized glass of beer; *een kleintje pils* is a small glass.

○ A *koffie* is black; *koffie verkeerd* (coffee 'wrong') is made with milk, similar to a caffe latte.

Treasure Hunt

During the Golden Age, Amsterdam was the world's warehouse, stuffed with riches from the far corners of the earth. The capital's cupboards are still stocked with all kinds of exotica (just look at that red-light gear!), as well as antiques, but you'll also find cutting-edge Dutch fashion and design.

Specialities & Souvenirs

Dutch fashion is all about cool, practical designs that don't get caught in bike spokes. Dutch-designed homewares bring a stylish touch to everyday objects. Antiques, art and vintage goodies also rank high on the local list. Popular gifts include tulip bulbs, Gouda cheese and bottles of *jenever* (Dutch gin). Blue-and-white Delft pottery is a widely available quality souvenir. And, of course, clogs, bongs and pot-leaf-logo T-shirts are in great supply.

Shopping Streets

The busiest shopping streets are Kalverstraat by the Dam and Leidsestraat, which leads into Leidseplein. Both are lined with department stores, such as Dutch retailers Hema and De Bijenkorf. The Old South's PC Hooftstraat lines up Chanel, Diesel, Gucci and other fancy fashion brands.

Boutiques & Antiques

At the top of the Jordaan, Haarlemmerstraat and Haarlemmerdijk are lined with hip boutiques and food shops. Just to the south, the Negen Straatjes (Nine Streets) offers a satisfying browse among offbeat, pint-sized shops.

Antique and art buffs should head for the Southern Canal Ring's Spiegel Quarter, along Spiegelgracht and Nieuwe Spiegelstraat.

Best Markets

Albert Cuypmarkt Vibrant street market spilling over with food, fashion and bargain finds. (p123)

Waterlooplein Flea Market Piles of curios for treasure hunters. (p151)

Noordermarkt It's morning bliss trawling for organic

MARIO SAVOIA/SHUTTERSTOCK ©

foods and vintage clothes. (p63)

Best Dutch Design

Hôtel Droog The famed collective is known for sly, playful, repurposed and re-invented homewares. (p163)

Frozen Fountain Amsterdam's best-known showcase of Dutch-designed furniture and homewares. (p75)

Hutspot Funky store giving emerging designers an opportunity to sell their work. (p131)

X Bank Dazzling displays change monthly. (p53)

Best Fashion

VLVT Up-and-coming Dutch-designed women's

fashion on chic Cornelis Schuytstraat. (p119)

Locals Locally designed fashion and accessories for men and women. (p53)

Vanilia Dutch label making limited-edition women's wear. (p77)

Best Souvenirs

Bloemenmarkt Bulbs, bulbs and more bulbs

fill Amsterdam's 'float-ing' flower market. (p85; pictured)

Mark Raven Grafiek Artsy, beyond-the-norm T-shirts and prints of the city. (p54)

Museum Shop at the Museumplein The one-stop shop for all your Rembrandt, Vermeer and Van Gogh items. (p114)

Treasure Hunt: Top Tips

○ Department stores and large shops gener-ally open seven days; some smaller shops close on Sunday and/or Monday.

○ Many shops stay open to 9pm Thursdays.

○ Useful words to know: *kassa* (cashier), *kort-ing* (discount) and *uitverkoop* (clearance sale).

Museums & Galleries

Amsterdam's world-class museums draw millions of visitors each year. The art collections take pride of place – you can't walk a kilometre here without bumping into a masterpiece. Canal-house museums are another local speciality. And the city has a fine assortment of oddball museums dedicated to everything from handbags to houseboats.

All the Art

The Dutch Masters helped spawn the prolific art collections around town. Seminal painters such as Johannes Vermeer, Frans Hals and Rembrandt van Rijn came along during the Golden Age when a new, bourgeois society of merchants and shopkeepers were spending money to brighten up their homes and workplaces with fresh paintings. The masters were there to meet the need, and their output from the era now fills the city's top museums.

Other Treasures

The Netherlands' maritime prowess during the Golden Age also filled the coffers of local institutions. Silver, porcelain and colonial knick-knacks picked up on distant voyages form the basis of collections in the Rijksmuseum, Amsterdam Museum, Het Scheepvaartmuseum and Tropenmuseum.

Canal-House Museums

There are two kinds: the first preserves the house as a living space, with sumptuous interiors that show how the richest locals lived once upon a time, as at Museum Van Loon. The other type uses the elegant structure as a backdrop for unique collections, such as the Kattenkabinet for cat art.

Best Art Museums

Rijksmuseum The Netherlands' top treasure house bursts with Rembrandts, Vermeers, Delftware and more. (p102; pictured)

Van Gogh Museum Hangs the world's largest collection of the tortured artist's vivid swirls. (p106)

ALEXANDER TOLSTYKH/SHUTTERSTOCK ©

Museum het Rembrandt-huis Immerse yourself in the old master's paint-spattered studio and handsome home. (p148)

Stedelijk Museum Renowned modern art from Picasso to Mondrian to Warhol. (p113)

Hermitage Amsterdam The satellite of Russia's Hermitage Museum features one-off, blockbuster exhibits. (p88)

Foam Changing photography exhibits by world-renowned shutterbugs. (p89)

Best History Museums

Anne Frank Huis The Secret Annexe and Anne's claustrophobic bedroom serve as chilling reminders of WWII. (p60)

Amsterdam Museum Whizz-bang exhibits take you through the twists and turns of Amsterdam's convoluted history. (p44)

Verzetsmuseum Learn about WWII Dutch resistance fighters during the Nazi occupation. (p155)

Museums & Galleries: Top Tips

○ Pre-book tickets for the big museums.

○ Many online tickets only have allocated time slots.

○ Queues are shortest during late afternoon and evening.

○ Friday, Saturday and Sunday are the busiest days.

○ Many hotels sell surcharge-free tickets to the big museums as a service to guests; ask your front-desk staff.

Show Time

Amsterdam supports a flourishing arts scene, with loads of big concert halls, theatres, cinemas, comedy clubs and other performance venues filled on a regular basis. Music fans are superbly catered for here, and there is a fervent subculture for just about every genre, especially jazz, classical, rock and avant-garde beats.

Music

Jazz is extremely popular, from far-out, improvisational stylings to more traditional notes. The grand Bimhuis (p162) is the big game in town, drawing visiting musicians from around the globe, though its vibe is more that of a funky little club. Smaller jazz venues abound and it's easy to find a live combo.

Amsterdam's classical-music scene, with top international orchestras, conductors and soloists crowding the agenda, is the envy of many European cities. Choose between the flawless Concertgebouw or dramatic Muziekgebouw aan 't IJ for the main shows.

Many of the city's clubs also host rock bands. Huge touring names often play smallish venues such as the Melkweg and Paradiso; it's a real treat to catch one of your favourites here.

Comedy & Theatre

Given that the Dutch are fine linguists and have a keen sense of humour, English-language comedy thrives in Amsterdam, especially around the Jordaan. Local theatre tends towards the edgy and experimental.

Cinema

Amsterdam's weather is fickle and, let's face it, even art lovers can overdose on museums. Luckily this town is a cinephile's heaven, with oodles of art-house cinemas. Numerous screenings are in English.

Best Rock

Paradiso One-time church that preaches a gospel of rock. (p96; pictured)

Melkweg Housed in a former dairy, it's Amsterdam's

SARAH COGHILL/LONELY PLANET ©

coolest club-gallery-cinema-concert hall. (p96)

OCCII A former squat that gives the night to edgy alternative bands. (p111)

De Nieuwe Anita Rock out by the stage behind the bookcase-concealed door. (p75)

Best Classical & Opera

Muziekgebouw aan 't IJ Stunning high-tech temple of the performing arts. (p162)

Concertgebouw World-renowned concert hall with superb acoustics. (p118)

Best Comedy & Theatre

Tobacco Theater Cabaret and theatre productions in

a former tobacco auction house. (p52)

Boom Chicago Laugh-out-loud improv-style comedy in the Jordaan. (p75)

Best Cinemas

EYE Film Institute The Netherlands' striking film

centre shows quality films of all kinds. (p168)

Pathé Tuschinskitheater Amsterdam's most famous cinema, with a sumptuous art-deco Amsterdam School interior. (p96)

Movies Amsterdam's oldest cinema dates from 1912. (p75)

Show Time: Top Tips

○ The **Last Minute Ticket Shop** (www.lastminuteticketshop.nl; ⊙online ticket sales from 10am on day of performance) sells same-day half-price tickets for concerts, performances and even club nights online. Events are handily marked 'LNP' (language no problem) if understanding Dutch isn't vital.

○ For events listings check I Amsterdam (www.iamsterdam.com); for movie screenings visit Film Ladder (www.filmladder.nl/amsterdam).

Canals

MATT MUNRO/LONELY PLANET ©

Amsterdammers have always known that their Canal Ring, built during the Golden Age, is extraordinary. Unesco made it official in 2010, when it listed the waterways as a World Heritage site. Today the city has 165 canals spanned by 1753 bridges – more than any other city in the world.

Best Views

Golden Bend Where the Golden Age magnates built their mansions along the regal Herengracht. (p85)

Reguliersgracht The 'canal of seven bridges' is one of Amsterdam's most photographed vistas. (p89)

Prinsengracht The liveliest of Amsterdam's inner canals, with cafes, shops and houseboats lining the quays.

Brouwersgracht Among very tough competition, Amsterdammers swear this is the city's most beautiful canal.

Best Canal-Related Museums

Het Grachtenhuis Inventive multimedia displays explain how the Canal Ring and its houses were built. (p66)

Houseboat Museum Discover how *gezellig* (cosy) houseboat living can be aboard this 1914 barge-turned-museum. (p68)

Best Canalside Drinking & Dining

De Belhamel At the head of the Herengracht, this superb restaurant's tables along the canal are an aphrodisiac. (p69)

Buffet van Odette Simple, creative cooking overlooking the Prinsengracht's crooked canal houses. (p92)

't Smalle Dock your boat right by the stone terrace of the 18th-century former *jenever* (Dutch gin) distillery. (p72)

Canals: Top Tips

∘ Virtually none of Amsterdam's canals have fences or barriers. Keep a close eye on young children.

∘ The **Canal Bus** (☎020-217 05 00; www.stromma.nl; hop-on, hop-off day pass €24.50, cruises €11.50-14.50, pedalos €10; ☉9am-6pm Mon-Wed, to 8pm Thu-Sun; ☎) provides a handy hop-on, hop-off service.

Cycling

MARK READ/LONELY PLANET ©

Bicycles are more common than cars in Amsterdam, and to roll like a local you'll need a two-wheeler. Rent one from the myriad outlets around town or from your accommodation, and the whole city becomes your playground. Cycling is the quintessential activity while visiting.

Journey Planning

Online journey planners include Fietsersbond (www.routeplanner.fietsersbond.nl), the official route planner of the Dutch Cyclists' Union. Holland Cycling (www.holland-cycling.com) has a wealth of up-to-date info such as bicycle-repair shops. Route You (www.routeyou.com) is good for scenic routes.

Road Rules

Helmets aren't compulsory but are recommended; most bike-hire places rent them out.

Amsterdam has over 500km of bike paths. Use the bicycle lane on the road's right-hand side, marked by white lines and bike symbols.

Cycle in the same direction as traffic and adhere to all traffic lights and signs.

Park only in designated bicycle racks

or risk the removal of your bike by the police.

Cycling on footpaths is illegal.

Best Cycling Spots

Vondelpark Urban oasis. (p110)

Eastern Islands Contemporary architecture. (p147)

Amsterdam Noord Windmills and farmland. (p165)

Cycling: Top Tips

○ Most bikes come with two locks: one for the front wheel (attach it to the bike frame), the other for the back. One of these locks should also be attached to a fixed structure (preferably a bike rack).

○ Cross tram rails at a sharp angle to avoid getting stuck.

For Free

RICHARD NEBESKY/LONELY PLANET ©

Although the costs of Amsterdam's accommodation and dining can mount up, there is a bright side. Not only is the entire Canal Ring a Unesco World Heritage site (effectively a free living museum), but there are plenty of things to do and see that are free (or virtually free).

Best Free Sights

Civic Guard Gallery Stroll through the monumental collection of portraits, from Golden Age to modern. (p41)

Rijksmuseum Gardens Even many locals don't know that the Renaissance and baroque gardens, with rose bushes, hedges and statues, are free and open to the public, including occasional sculpture exhibitions. (p102)

Begijnhof Explore the 14th-century hidden courtyard and its clandestine churches. (p38)

Stadsarchief You never know what treasures you'll find in the vaults of the city's archives. (p90)

Albert Cuypmarkt Amsterdam's busiest market; it and the city's many other bazaars are all free to browse. (p123)

ARCAM A fascinating look at Amsterdam's architecture – past, present and future. (p157)

Kunststad Wander through these vast artist studios in Amsterdam Noord. (p167)

NEMO Science Museum roof terrace One of the best views of Amsterdam extends from the roof of this landmark building. (p155)

Best Free Entertainment

Concertgebouw Sharpen your elbows to get in for Wednesday's lunchtime concert (September to June), often a public rehearsal for the performance later that evening. (p118)

Muziektheater Free classical concerts fill the air during lunch most Tuesdays from September to May. (p162)

Bimhuis Jazz sessions hot up the revered venue on Tuesday nights. (p162; pictured above, trumpeter Ack van Rooyen performing at Bimhuis)

Openluchttheater Vondelpark's outdoor theatre puts on concerts and kids' shows throughout summer. (p111)

EYE Film Institute Has pods in the basement where you can watch free films. (p168)

King's Day The ultimate party, this is one of many festivals and events that are free. (p133)

Under the Radar

Throughout Amsterdam there are many opportunities to discover lesser-known attractions. The compact size of the Dutch capital means you don't have to venture far beyond its major tourist hubs to explore fascinating local neighbourhoods tucked away from the beaten track.

ERIK LAAN/SHUTTERSTOCK ©

Canal Cruise Alternatives

Getting out on the water gives you a different perspective of Amsterdam's canals, with plenty of alternatives to sightseeing cruises. Canal tours with a twist include the laid-back, irreverent outings run by **Those Dam Boat Guys** (www.thosedamboatguys.com). Rederij Lampedusa (p161) provides a poignant insight into Amsterdam's immigration aboard a former refugee boat. You can even help clean Amsterdam's waterways yourself by 'plastic fishing' from boats made from retrieved and recycled plastic waste with **Plastic Whale** (www.plasticwhale.com). Another great way to explore is to rent your own zero-emission electric canal boat from companies such as Boaty (p125).

Best Under-the-Radar Museums & Galleries

Below the Surface Staggering array of archaeological finds unearthed during the construction of the North–South metro line. (p45)

Kunststad Hundreds of artists work and exhibit in Amsterdam Noord at this 'Art City'. (p167)

Fashion for Good Find out where your clothes come from at this sustainable fashion museum. (p46)

Kattenkabinet Feline art in a beautiful Golden Bend canal house. (p85)

Best Under-the-Radar Parks

Westerpark Leafy expanse adjacent to the former gasworks that now house the Westergasfabriek cultural complex (pictured). (p81)

Sarphatipark Local favourite for picnics in the village-like neighbourhood of De Pijp. (p123)

Oosterpark Sprawling green park in Amsterdam's multicultural east. (p140)

Park Frankendael Beautiful formal gardens of a former country estate mansion. (p140)

For Kids

Breathe easy: you've landed in one of Europe's most kid-friendly cities. The famous Dutch tolerance extends to children and Amsterdammers are cheerfully accommodating to them. You'll find that virtually all quarters of the city – except the Red Light District, of course – are fair game for the younger set.

WILL SALTER/LONELY PLANET ©
ARCHITECT: RENZO PIANO

Best Activities for Kids

NEMO Kid-focused, hands-on science labs inside and a terrace with a splashy summer water feature outside. (p155; pictured)

Het Scheepvaartmuseum Climb aboard the full-scale, 17th-century replica ship and check out the cannons. (p155)

Tropenmuseum Spend the afternoon learning to yodel, sitting in a yurt or travelling via otherworldly exhibits. (p136)

Vondelpark Space-age slides at the western end, playground in the middle, duck ponds throughout. (p110)

Artis Royal Zoo Monkeys, big cats, shimmying fish and a planetarium provide all the requisite thrills. (p154)

Centrale Bibliotheek Amsterdam Has a whole children's floor with story times, reading lounges and books in English. (p157)

Micropia The world's first microbe museum has a wall of poop, a kissing meter and other inventive exhibits. (p154)

Best Kids' Shops

Het Oud-Hollandsch Snoepwinkeltje Stocks jar after jar of Dutch penny sweets. (p76)

Mechanisch Speelgoed Nostalgic wind-up toys. (p79)

Tinkerbell Toy shop with a mechanical bear blowing bubbles out front. (p99)

For Kids: Top Tips

○ 'Child' is defined as under 18 years. But at many tourist sites, the cut-off age for free or reduced rates is 12. Some sights may only provide free entry to children under six.

○ Most bike-rental shops hire bikes with baby or child seats.

○ Many higher-end hotels arrange baby-sitting services for a fee.

LGBTIQ+

NANCY BEIJERSBERGEN/SHUTTERSTOCK ©

To call Amsterdam a gay capital doesn't express just how welcoming and open the scene is here. The Netherlands was the first country to legalise same-sex marriage (in 2001), so it's no surprise that Amsterdam's gay scene is among the world's largest.

Party Zones

Five hubs party hardest. **Warmoesstraat** in the Red Light District hosts the infamous, kink-filled leather and fetish bars. Nearby on the upper end of the **Zeedijk** crowds spill onto laid-back bar terraces.

In the Southern Canal Ring, the area around **Rembrandtplein** (aka the 'Amstel area') has traditional pubs and brown cafes, some with a campy bent. Leidseplein has a smattering of high-action clubs along **Kerkstraat**.

And **Reguliersdwarsstraat**, located one street down from the flower market, draws the beautiful crowd at its trendy, fickle hot spots.

Top Tips

Gay Amsterdam (www.gayamsterdam. com) lists hotels, shops and clubs, and provides maps.

Information kiosk/souvenir shop **Pink Point** (📞020-428 10 70; www.pinkpoint. nl; Westermarkt; 🕐10.30am-6pm Mon-Sat, noon-6pm Sun; 🚋13/17 Westermarkt) has details of parties, events and social groups.

Pride Amsterdam (www.pride.amsterdam; 🕐late Jul-early Aug) features the world's only waterborne Pride parade (pictured).

Best LGBTIQ+ Hangouts

't Mandje Amsterdam's oldest gay bar is a trinket-covered beauty. (p52)

Montmartre Legendary bar where Dutch ballads and old top-40 hits tear the roof off. (p96)

De Trut A Sunday fixture on the scene. (p74)

Taboo Bar Drag shows and party games. (p95)

Four Perfect Days

Day 1

NATTEE CHALERMTIRAGOOL/SHUTTERSTOCK ©
"SCULPTURE 'OISEAU LUNAIRE' BY JOAN MIRÓ

Begin by viewing the master-pieces at the Museum Quarter's **Rijksmuseum** (pictured; p102) and **Van Gogh Museum** (p106). Modern-art buffs might want to swap one for the **Stedelijk Museum** (p113).

Explore the secret courtyard and gardens at the **Begijnhof** (p38) in the in the Medieval Centre. Stroll to the **Dam** (p45), where the **Royal Palace** (p36) and **Nieuwe Kerk** (p44) provide a dose of Dutch history. Bend over to sip your *jenever* (Dutch gin) like a local at **Wynand Fockink** (p41).

Venture into the Red Light District for an eye-popping look at Amsterdam's wild side. Then settle in to a brown cafe (traditional Dutch pub), such as **IIn 't Aepjen** (p49).

Day 2

KJELL LENNES/SHUTTERSTOCK ©

Browse Amsterdam's largest street market, De Pijp's **Albert Cuypmarkt** (p123). Then get shaken up, heated up and 'bottled' like a beer at the **Heineken Experience** (p125).

Cross into the Southern Canal Ring to check out the opulent canal-house lifestyle at **Museum Van Loon** (p89), feline art at the **Kattenkabinet** (p85), and bulbs galore at the **Bloemenmarkt** (p85).

After dark, par-tee at hyper-active, neon-lit **Leidseplein** (pictured; p91), surrounded by good-time clubs and brown cafes (traditional Dutch pubs). **Paradiso** (p96) and **Melk-weg** (p96) host the coolest agendas.

Day 3

WILL SALTER/LONELY PLANET ©

Day 4

ALEXANDER TOLSTYKH/SHUTTERSTOCK ©

Take a spin around Amsterdam's beloved **Vondelpark** (pictured; p110). It's easy to explore via a morning jaunt; all the better if you have a bicycle to zip by the ponds, gardens and sculptures.

Immerse yourself in the Western Canal Ring's **Negen Straatjes** (p63), a noughts-and-crosses board of speciality shops. At the nearby **Anne Frank Huis** (p60), the claustro-phobic rooms give an all-too-real feel for Anne's life in hiding, as does seeing her diary.

Spend the evening in the Jordaan, the chummy district embodying the Amsterdam of yore. Hoist a glass on a canal-side terrace at **'t Smalle** (p72) or quaff beers at heaps of other *gezellig* (cosy) haunts.

Mosey through **Waterlooplein Flea Market** (pictured; p151) in Nieuwmarkt before visiting Rembrandt's studio at the **Museum het Rembrandthuis** (p148). Discover Resistance history at the **Verzetsmuseum** (p155), or sea treasures at **Het Scheepvaartmuseum** (p155).

Cross the the IJ River to up-and-coming Amsterdam Noord. Catch cinematic exhibits at the **EYE Film Institute** (p168) and artists in the **Kunststad** (p167) studios. Ascend **A'DAM Tower** (p167) for panoramic views.

Back on the city side of the IJ, enjoy a drink at **De Ysbreeker** (p143), overlooking the Amstel river.

Need to Know

For detailed information, see Survival Guide (p173)

Currency
Euro (€)

Language
Dutch

Visas
Generally not required for stays up to 90 days; from 2022, non-EU nationals need ETIAS pre-authorisation.

Money
ATMs widely available. Some establishments accept only cash, or only cards.

Mobile Phones
Ask your home provider about an international plan. Alternatively, local prepaid SIM cards are widely available.

Time
Central European Time (GMT/UTC plus one hour).

Tipping
Leave 5% to 10% for a cafe snack (or round up to the next euro), 10% or so for a restaurant meal. Tip taxi drivers 5% to 10%.

Daily Budget

Budget: Less than €130
Dorm bed: €25–60
Supermarkets and lunchtime specials for food: €20
Boom Chicago late-night show ticket: €15
Bike hire per day: €12

Midrange: €130–300
Double room: from €150
Three-course dinner in casual restaurant: €40
Concertgebouw ticket: €40
Canal Bus day pass: €21

Top end: More than €300
Four-star hotel double room: from €250
Five-course dinner in top restaurant: from €80
Private canal-boat rental for two hours: from €90

Advance Planning

Four months before Book your accommodation, especially if you're visiting in summer or on a weekend.

Two months before Check club and performing-arts calendars and buy tickets for anything that looks appealing.

Two weeks before Make dinner reservations at your must-eat restaurants, reserve walking or cycling tours, and purchase tickets online to popular attractions like the Van Gogh Museum, Anne Frank Huis and Rijksmuseum.

Arriving in Amsterdam

✈ From Schiphol International Airport

Trains to Centraal Station depart every 10 minutes or so from 6am to 12.30am, hourly at other times; the 15-minute trip costs €4.50. Taxis cost €39.

🚇 From Centraal Station

In central Amsterdam with many tram and metro lines connecting it to the rest of the city; taxis queue near the front entrance (towards the west side).

🚌 From Bus Stations

Eurolines buses use Duivendrecht station, south of the centre; FlixBus uses Sloterdijk station, west of the centre. Both are linked to Centraal by train and metro.

Getting Around

GVB passes in chip-card form are the most convenient option for public transport.

🚶 Walking

Central Amsterdam is easily covered by foot.

🚲 Bicycle

Rental companies are everywhere; bikes cost about €12 daily.

🚊 Tram

Frequent and ubiquitous, operating between 6am and 12.30am.

🚌 Bus & Metro

Primarily serve outer districts; metro 52 links Amsterdam Noord with the World Trade Centre in the south via the city centre and De Pijp.

⛴ Ferry

Free ferries to Amsterdam Noord depart from docks behind Centraal Station.

Amsterdam Neighbourhoods

Medieval Centre & Red Light District (p35)
Amsterdam's medieval core mixes fairy-tale Golden Age buildings, *bruin cafés* and the lurid Red Light District.

Jordaan & the Western Canal Ring (p59)
The Jordaan teems with cosy pubs and lanes ideal for getting lost. The Western Canal Ring unfurls quirky boutiques and waterside cafés.

Anne Frank Huis ⊙

Royal Palace ⊙
(Koninklijk Paleis)

Begijnhof ⊙

Vondelpark ⊙
Rijksmuseum ⊙
Van Gogh Museum ⊙

Vondelpark & the South (p101)
Vondelpark is a green lung with personality, adjacent to the genteel Old South, home to Amsterdam's grandest museums.

Southern Canal Ring (p83)
By day, visit the city's less-heralded museums. By night, party at the clubs around Leidseplein and Rembrandtplein.

Amsterdam Noord (p165)
Once industrial, Amsterdam's north is now home to some of the city's most cutting-edge creative venues.

Nieuwmarkt, Plantage & the Eastern Islands (p147)
See Rembrandt's studio and Amsterdam's Jewish heritage in Nieuwmarkt, and gardens and a beery windmill in the Plantage.

Museum het Rembrandthuis

Tropenmuseum

Oosterpark & East of the Amstel (p135)
One of the city's most culturally diverse areas, with Moroccan and Turkish enclaves and some great bars and restaurants.

De Pijp (p121)
Ethnic meets trendy in this recently gentrified neighbourhood, best sampled at the colourful Albert Cuypmarkt and multicultural eateries that surround it.

Explore
Amsterdam

Pub exterior, Red Light District JON CHICA/SHUTTERSTOCK ©

Medieval Centre & Red Light District

Amsterdam's oldest quarter is remarkably preserved, looking much as it did in its Golden Age heyday. It's the busiest part of town for visitors. While some come to see the Royal Palace and Oude Kerk, others make a beeline for the coffeeshops and Red Light District.

The Short List

○ **Amsterdam Museum (p44)** *Time-travelling through seven pivotal periods across a millennia of history at this high-tech museum.*

○ **Royal Palace (p36)** *Marvelling at the chandeliered opulence at the city's landmark palace.*

○ **Begijnhof (p38)** *Pushing open the door to find this tranquil courtyard's hidden gardens and churches.*

○ **Vleminckx (p47)** *Biting into crisp golden frites (fries) slathered in mayonnaise, curry or peanut sauce from Amsterdam's best frites stand.*

○ **Wynand Fockink (p41)** *Bowling up to this 17th-century tasting house to knock back a jenever (Dutch gin) or taking a pre-booked weekend tour.*

Getting There & Around

🚋 The majority of the city's 15 tram lines go through the neighbourhood en route to Centraal Station.

Ⓜ Metros travel from Centraal to Amsterdam's outer neighbourhoods, and to Amsterdam Noord and Station Zuid via Rokin in the Medieval Centre.

⚓ Free ferries to Amsterdam Noord depart from the piers behind Centraal Station.

Neighbourhood Map on p42

Royal Palace (p36) ANIBAL TREJO/SHUTTERSTOCK ©

Top Experience 📷

Marvel at the Opulence of the Royal Palace (Koninklijk Paleis)

Today's Royal Palace began life as a glorified town hall and was completed in 1665. Its architect, Jacob van Campen, spared no expense to display Amsterdam's wealth in a way that rivalled the grandest European buildings of the day. The result is opulence on a big scale. It's worth seeing the exterior at night, when it is dramatically floodlit.

◉ MAP P42, B5

☎ 020-522 61 61

www.paleisamsterdam.nl

adult/child €10/free

🕐 10am-5pm

🚊 4/14/24 Dam

A King's Residence

Officially, the Dutch king, King Willem-Alexander, lives in this landmark **palace** and pays a symbolic rent, though his actual residence is in Den Haag. If he's not here in Amsterdam, visitors have the opportunity to come in and wander around the monumental building.

The 1st Floor

Most of the rooms spread over the **1st floor**, which is awash in chandeliers (51 shiners in total), along with damasks, gilded clocks, and some spectacular paintings by artists including Ferdinand Bol and Jacob de Wit. The great *burgerzaal* (citizens' hall) that occupies the heart of the building was envisioned as a schematic of the world, with Amsterdam as its centre. Check out the maps inlaid in the floor; they show the eastern and western hemispheres, with a 1654 celestial map in the middle.

Empire-style Decor

In 1808 the building became the palace of King Louis, Napoleon Bonaparte's brother. In a classic slip-up in the new lingo, French-born Louis told his subjects here that he was the 'rabbit' (*konijn*) of Holland, when he actually meant 'king' (*koning*, which had the old spelling variation *konink*). Napoleon dismissed him two years later. Louis left behind about 1000 pieces of Empire-style furniture and decorative artworks. As a result, the palace now holds one of the world's largest **collections** from the period.

★ **Top Tips**

○ The Royal Palace is still used for state functions and often closes for such events, especially during April, May, November and December. The schedule is posted on the website.

○ When you enter, be sure to pick up the free audioguide, which vividly details the palace's main features.

✕ **Take a Break**

Pick up traditional Dutch *stroopwafels* (caramel syrup-filled waffles) at the shiny food hall inside Magna Plaza (p55).

Sip *jenever* (Dutch gin) amid gorgeous blue-and-white Delft tiles and timber panelling at **De Blauwe Parade** (www.deblauweparade. com; Nieuwezijds Voorburgwal 178; ⏰4pm-midnight; ☎; 🚊2/11/12/13/17 Dam).

Top Experience 📷

Step into a Story Book at Begijnhof

You walk up to the unassuming door, push it open and voila – a hidden courtyard of tiny houses and gardens opens up before you. The 14th-century Begijnhof is not a secret these days, but somehow it remains a surreal oasis of peace in the city's midst.

◎ MAP P42, B7

www.nicolaas-parochie.nl

admission free

🕘 9am-5pm

🚊 2/11/12 Spui

History

The **Beguines** were a Catholic order of unmarried or widowed women who lived a religious life without taking monastic vows. The Begijnhof was their convent of sorts. The last true Beguine died in 1971.

Begijnhof Kapel

One of two churches hidden in the *hof* (courtyard), the 1671 **Begijnhof Kapel** (www.begijnhof kapelamsterdam.nl; Begijnhof 30; ⏰1-6.30pm Mon, 9am-6.30pm Tue-Fri, 9am-6pm Sat & Sun; 🚊2/11/12 Spui) is a 'clandestine' chapel where the Beguines were forced to worship after the Calvinists took away their Gothic church. Go through the dog-leg entrance to find marble columns, stained-glass windows and murals commemorating the Miracle of Amsterdam. (In short: in 1345 the final sacrament was administered to a dying man, but he was unable to keep down the communion wafer and brought it back up. Here's the miracle part: when the vomit was thrown on the fire, the wafer would not burn. Yes, it's all depicted in wall paintings.)

Engelse Kerk

The other church is known as the **Engelse Kerk** (English Church; www.ercadam.nl; Begijnhof 48; ⏰9am-5pm; 🚊2/11/12 Spui), built around 1392. It was eventually rented out to the local community of English and Scottish Presbyterian refugees – including the Pilgrim Fathers – and it still serves as the city's Presbyterian church. Look for pulpit panels by Piet Mondrian, in a figurative phase. Note that as this church is still in frequent use, it's sometimes closed to visitors.

Houten Huis

Look out, too, for the **Houten Huis** (Wooden House; Begijnhof 34; 🚊2/11/12 Spui) at No 34. It dates from around 1465, making it the oldest preserved wooden house in the Netherlands.

★ Top Tips

○ Look for a wooden door on the Spui's north side, east of the American Book Center, to find another entrance to the Begijnhof near the Houten Huis.

○ Today, 105 single women still live in the Begijnhof. Visitors are asked to be respectful, not to eat, drink, smoke (any substance), litter or photograph the houses, and to keep noise to a minimum.

✗ Take a Break

Dine on classic Dutch dishes at quaint Tomaz (p49).

Stop by *bruin café* **Pilsener Club** (Begijnensteeg 4; ⏰noon-1am Mon-Thu, to 2am Fri & Sat; 🚊2/11/12 Spui) for a frothy beer.

Walking Tour 🚶

Cheese, Gin & Monuments

This tour is a hit parade of Amsterdam's favourite foods and historic sights. Swoop through the Western Canals and City Centre, gobbling up traditional kaas (cheese), haring (herring) and jenever (gin) in between stops at the city's birthplace, its Royal Palace and a Golden Age art cache. It's a big bite of Amsterdam in under two hours. The best time to trek is early afternoon, when opening times for the sights and bars coincide.

Walk Facts

Start De Kaaskamer; 1/2/5 Spui

End Wynand Fockink; 4/9/16/24 Dam

Length 2km; 1½ to two hours with stops

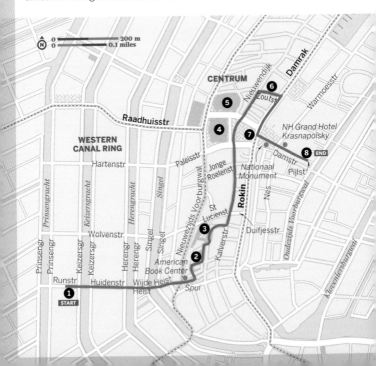

❶ De Kaaskamer

The Dutch eat more than 14kg of cheese per person annually and it appears much of that hunky goodness is sold right here in **De Kaaskamer** (www.kaaskamer.nl; Runstraat 7; ⏰noon-6pm Mon, 9am-6pm Tue-Fri, 9am-5pm Sat, noon-5pm Sun; 🚋2/11/12 Spui). Wheels of Gouda, Edam and other locally made types stack up to the rafters. Get a wedge to go.

❷ Begijnhof

On the Spui, just past the American Book Center, is a humble wood door. Push it open and behold the hidden community known as the **Begijnhof** (p38) surrounding two historic churches and gardens. Cross the courtyard to the other entrance.

❸ Civic Guard Gallery

From the Begijnhof turn north and walk a short distance to the **Civic Guard Gallery** (Kalverstraat 92; admission free; ⏰10am-5pm; 🚋2/11/12 Spui). Paintings of stern folks in ruffled collars stare down from the walls. Cross the gallery and depart through the Amsterdam Museum's courtyard restaurant onto Kalverstraat.

❹ Royal Palace

Kalverstraat deposits you by the **Royal Palace** (p36), King Willem-Alexander's pad, though he's rarely here, preferring Den Haag for his digs. The sumptuous interior deserves a look.

❺ Nieuwe Kerk

The palace's neighbour is the **Nieuwe Kerk** (p44), the stage for Dutch coronations. After admiring its mightiness, get onto crowded Nieuwendijk, which you'll walk for a short while until you dive down Zoutsteeg.

❻ Rob Wigboldus Vishandel

C'mon, stop being shy about eating raw fish. Try the famed Dutch herring at **Rob Wigboldus Vishandel** (p49), a teeny three-table shop. Once sated, depart Zoutsteeg onto Damrak.

❼ Dam

Cross Damrak so you're on the Nationaal Monument side of the **Dam** (p45) – Amsterdam's birthplace. Wade through the sea of bikes to see the urns behind the monument, which hold earth from East Indies war cemeteries. Now follow the street leading behind the NH Grand Hotel Krasnapolsky.

❽ Wynand Fockink

'Sshh, the *jenever* is resting', says the admonition over the door at **Wynand Fockink** (📞020-639 26 95; www.wynand-fockink.nl; Pijlsteeg 31; tours €17.50; ⏰tasting tavern 2-9pm daily, tours 3pm, 4.30pm, 6pm & 7.30pm Sat & Sun; 🚋4/14/24 Dam). The Dutch-gin maker's tasting room dates from 1679. The barkeep will pour your drink to the brim, so do like the locals to prevent spillage: lean over it and sip without lifting.

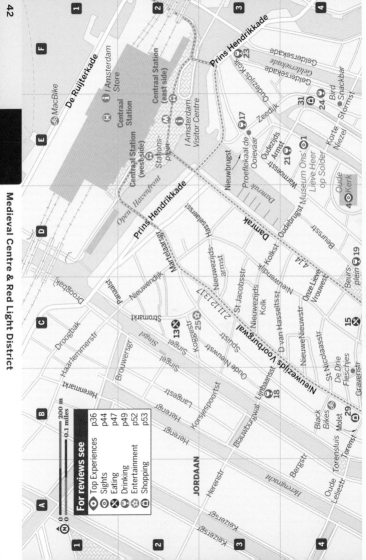

Medieval Centre & Red Light District

For reviews see

Top Experiences p36
◇ Sights p44
✕ Eating p47
🍷 Drinking p49
🎭 Entertainment p52
🛍 Shopping p53

200 m
0.1 miles

De Ruijterkade

Open Havenfront

Prins Hendrikkade

Prins Hendrikkade

i Amsterdam Store

Centraal Station

Centraal Station (east side)

Centraal Station (west side)

Stations-plein

i Amsterdam Visitor Centre

MacBike

Droogbak

Droogbak

Haarlemmerstr

Herengr

Herengr

Keizersgr

JORDAAN

Herenstr

Herengracht

Keizersgr

Brouwersgr

Singel

Singel

Singel

Oude Nieuwstr

Spuistr

Nieuwendijk

Martelaarsg

Nieuwezijds Kolk

Nieuwezijds Voorburgwal

Nieuwendijk

Stromarkt

Nieuwe Nieuwstr

Langestr

Korsjespoortstr

Blauwburgwal

Oude Leliestr

Torensluis

Bergstr

Torenstr

Molst

Black Bikes

De Drie Fleschjes

Gravenstr

St Nicolaasstr

Onze Lieve Vrouwestr

D van Hasseltsst

St Jacobsstr

Kolk

Nieuwezijds Armsteeg

Hasselaerst

Damrak

Damrak

Nieuwbrugst

Oudebrugst

Beurspl

Beursstr

Beurspassage

Warmoesstr

Oudezijds Armsteeg

Proeflokaal de Ooievaar

Museum Ons' Lieve Heer op Solder

Oude Kerk

Zeedijk

Korte Niezel

Oudezijds Kolk

Geldersekade

Geldersekade

Geldersekade

Bird Snackbar

Stormst

23

17

21

1

4

31

24

19

15

29

18

25

13

2 11 12 13 17

4 14

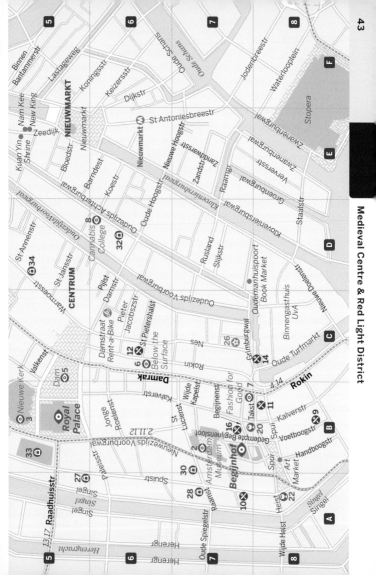

F
E
D
C
B
A

5
6
7
8

Binnen Bantammerstr
Lastageweg
Binnen
Nam Kee
New King
Kuan Yin
Shrine
Zeedijk

NIEUWMARKT

Koningsstr
Keizersstr
Dijkstr
Oude Schans

Oude Schans

Jodenbreestr
Waterlooplein

Bloedstr
Barndest
Koestr
Nieuwmarkt

St Antoniesbreestr
Nieuwe Hoogstr
Zandstr
Zanddwarsstr

Raamgr

Zwanenburgwal
Zwanenburgwal

Verversstr

Stopera

Oudezijds Voorburgwal
Oudezijds Achterburgwal

Oude Hoogstr
Kloveniersburgwal

Groenburgwal
Staalstr
Kloveniersburgwal

St Annenstr
34
St Jansstr

CENTRUM
Warmoesstr

Pijlst
Damstr
Cannabis College
8
32

Oudezijds Voorburgwal

Rusland
Slijkstr

Nieuwe Doelenstr

Oudemanhuispoort
Book Market

Binnengasthuis
UVA

Damstraat Rent-a-Bike
Pieter Jacobszstr
St Pietershalst
Below the Surface
12
6

Nes

26

Grimburgwal
Oude Turfmarkt

14

Dam
5

Damrak
Rokin
Rokin
4.14

Jonge Roelenst
Wijde Kapelst
Kalverstr
7
Gapid
Fashion for
11
Takst
20
16

Kalverstr
Voetboogstr
9

Nieuwe Kerk
Valkenst
3
Royal Palace

33

Paleisstr
Lijnbaanst
Nieuwezijds Voorburgwal
Spuistr
30
2
Amsterdam Museum
Gedempte Begijnensloot
Begijnhof
Spui
Spui
Art Market
Handboogstr
Heist
22

27
28
Singel
Singel
Raamst

13.17 Raadhuisstr

Herengracht
Oude Spiegelstr
Herengr
Herengr
Wijde Heist
Singel
Singel

2.11.12

10

5
6
7
8

Sights

Museum Ons' Lieve Heer op Solder

MUSEUM

1 ⊙ MAP P42, E4

Within what looks like an ordinary canal house is an entire Catholic church. Ons' Lieve Heer op Solder (Our Dear Lord in the Attic) was built in the mid-1600s in defiance of the Calvinists. Inside you'll see labyrinthine staircases, rich artworks, period decor and the soaring, two-storey church itself. (☏020-624 66 04; www.opsolder.nl; Oudezijds Voorburgwal 38; adult/child €12.50/6; ⊙10am-6pm Mon-Sat, from 1pm Sun; ☐4/14/24 Dam)

Amsterdam Museum

MUSEUM

2 ⊙ MAP P42, B7

Entrepreneurship, free thinking, citizenship and creativity are the four cornerstones of the multi-media DNA exhibit at this riveting museum, which splits Amsterdam's history into seven key periods, comprehensively described by audioguides (included in admission). Unlike at many of the city's museums, crowds are rare. It's reached via the arcade containing the free Civic Guard Gallery (p41) off Kalverstraat 92. (☏020-523 18 22; www.amsterdammuseum.nl; Gedempte Begijnensloot; adult/child €15/free; ⊙10am-5pm; ☐2/11/12 Spui)

Nieuwe Kerk

CHURCH

3 ⊙ MAP P42, B5

This 15th-century late-Gothic basilica is only 'new' in relation to the Oude Kerk – the city's Old Church, dating from 1306. A few monumental items dominate the otherwise spartan interior – a magnificent carved oak chancel, a bronze choir screen, a massive organ and enormous stained-glass windows. It's the site of royal investitures and weddings; the building is otherwise used for art exhibitions and concerts. Opening times and prices can vary depending on what's going on. An audioguide costs €2. (New Church; ☏020-626 81 68; www.nieuwekerk.nl; Dam; adult/child €12.50/free; ⊙10am-6pm; ☐2/11/12/13/17 Dam)

Oude Kerk

CHURCH

4 ⊙ MAP P42, D4

Dating from 1306, the Oude Kerk is Amsterdam's oldest surviving building. It's also an intriguing moral contradiction: a church surrounded by active Red Light District windows. Inside, check out the stunning Vater-Müller organ, the naughty 15th-century carvings on the choir stalls, and famous Amsterdammers' tombstones in the floor (including Rembrandt's wife, Saskia van Uylenburgh). Regular art exhibitions take place in the church; you can also climb the **tower** (Oudekerkstoren; www.westertoren amsterdam.nl; Oudekerksplein;

tour €9; ◷1-7pm Mon-Sat Apr-Oct; 🚊4/14/24 Dam) on a guided tour. Church admission is by credit/debit card only. (Old Church; 📞020-625 82 84; www.oudekerk.nl; Oudekerksplein; adult/child €12/free; ◷10am-6pm Mon-Sat, 1-5.30pm Sun; 🚊4/14/24 Dam)

Dam   SQUARE

5 ◉ MAP P42, C5

This square is the very spot where Amsterdam was founded around 1270. Today pigeons, tourists, buskers and the occasional funfair (complete with Ferris wheel) take over the grounds. It's still a national gathering spot, and if there's a major speech or demonstration it's held here. (🚊4/14/24 Dam)

Below the Surface   GALLERY

6 ◉ MAP P42, C6

During the construction of Amsterdam's 2018-opened Noord/Zuidlijn (North–South metro line), more than 134,000 archaeological finds were unearthed from beneath the streets and waterways. Now 9500 of them dating as far back as 2400 BC are stunningly displayed in glass cases between Rokin metro station's escalators (visitors need a valid public transport ticket). Transport, craft and industry, buildings and interiors feature at the southern entrance. Objects at the northern entrance span science, communications, weapons, armour, recreation, personal items and clothing. (www.belowthesurface.amsterdam; Rokin metro station)

Dam

Red Light District Clean-Up

Since 2007 city officials have reduced the number of Red Light windows in an effort to clean up the Red Light District. They claim it's not about morals but about crime: pimps, traffickers and money launderers have entered the scene and set the neighbourhood on a downward spiral. Opponents point to a growing conservatism and say the government is using crime as an excuse because it doesn't like Amsterdam's reputation for sin.

To date, some 300 windows remain, down from 482. Scores of sex workers and their supporters have protested against the closures: the concern is that closing the windows simply forces sex workers to relocate to less safe environments. A buy-back project to replace windows with studios and local shops was largely unsuccessful, resulting in tourist-driven businesses (eg cheap souvenir shops) filling the gaps. However, from 2020, the city has banned guided tours along the Red Light District's windows (guided tours in the rest of the city centre are still allowed to operate, but require tour guides to have a special permit and abide by relevant rules).

Other initiatives for changing the face of the area include the introduction of festivals such as the **Red Light Jazz Festival** (www.redlightjazz.com; ⊘early Jun).

Fashion for Good   MUSEUM

7 ⊚ MAP P42, B7

The world's first sustainable fashion museum delves into the history of fashion, the latest industry technology and innovation, and the stories behind day-to-day clothing, such as the T-shirt. The colourful and interactive exhibition may make you think twice about your own consumer behaviour, highlighting, for example, that garments travel an average of 14,000km and are handled by 100 people before you buy them. Visitors leave with a personalised 'sustainable fashion action plan', encouraging you to make environmentally conscious fashion choices. (📞020-261 96 80; www.fashionforgood.com; Rokin 102; admission free; ⊘11am-7pm Mon-Fri, to 6pm Sat & Sun; ⓂRokin, 🚊4/14/24 Rokin)

Cannabis College   CULTURAL CENTRE

8 ⊚ MAP P42, D6

This nonprofit centre offers visitors tips and tricks for having a positive smoking experience and provides the low-down on local cannabis laws. There are educational displays and a library. Staff can provide maps and advice on where to find coffeeshops that

sell organic weed and shops that are good for newbies. T-shirts, stickers, postcards and a few other trinkets with the logo are for sale, too. (☎020-423 44 20; www.cannabiscollege.com; Oudezijds Achterburgwal 124; ⏰11am-7pm; 🚊4/14/24 Dam)

Eating

Vleminckx
FAST FOOD €

9 🍴 MAP P42, B8

Frying up *frites* (fries) since 1887, Amsterdam's best *friterie* has been based at this hole-in-the-wall takeaway shack near the Spui since 1957. The standard order of perfectly cooked crispy, fluffy *frites* is smothered in mayonnaise, though its 28 sauces also include apple, green pepper, ketchup, peanut, sambal and mustard. Queues almost always stretch down the block, but they move fast. (www.vleminckxdesausmeester.nl; Voetboogstraat 33; fries €3-5, sauces €0.70; ⏰noon-7pm Mon, 11am-7pm Tue-Wed & Fri-Sun, 11am-8pm Thu; 🚊2/11/12 Koningsplein)

D'Vijff Vlieghen
DUTCH €€

10 🍴 MAP P42, A7

Spread across five 17th-century canal houses, the 'Five Flies' is a jewel. Old-wood dining rooms overflow with character, featuring Delft Blue tiles and original works by Rembrandt; chairs have copper plates inscribed with the names of famous guests (Walt Disney, Mick Jagger...). Exquisite dishes range from smoked goose breast with apple to roast veal with turnips with Dutch crab mayonnaise. (☎020-530 40 60; www.vijffvliegen. nl; Spuistraat 294-302; mains €19.50-26.50; ⏰6-10pm; 🚊2/11/12 Spui)

Gartine
CAFE €

11 🍴 MAP P42, B8

Gartine is magical, from its covert location in an alley off busy Kalverstraat to its mismatched antique tableware and its sublime breakfast pastries (including a dark-chocolate, honey and raspberry soufflé), sandwiches and salads (made from produce grown in its garden plot and eggs from its chickens). The sweet-and-savoury high tea, from 2pm to 5pm, is a treat. (☎020-320 41 32; www.gartine.nl; Taksteeg 7; dishes €6.50-15, high tea €18-25.50; ⏰10am-6pm Wed-Sat; 🍴; MRokin, 🚊4/14/24 Rokin)

Ron Gastrobar Downtown
INDONESIAN €€

12 🍴 MAP P42, C6

Beneath a striking curved glass-and-metal ceiling, superstar chef Ron Blaauw showcases cutting-edge Indonesian cuisine: *saté kambing* (grilled goat skewers with peanut sauce), *udang peteh* (shrimp with bitter beans in coconut sauce) and *bebek mendoan* (slow-cooked duck with tempeh and green-sambal mayo). Downstairs, the lush jungle-themed bar serves Indonesian-inspired cocktails and morphs into a club

on Fridays and Saturday nights.
(📞020-790 03 22; www.rongastrobar
indonesia.nl; Rokin 49; mains €17.50-
27, rijsttafel per person €39.50;
🕑noon-10pm Tue-Thu, to 11pm Fri-
Sun; 🛜; Ⓜ Rokin, 🚊4/14/24 Rokin)

De Silveren Spiegel   DUTCH €€€

13 🍴 MAP P42, C2

Hung with replicas of Old Masters,
the 'Silver Mirror' is an exceedingly
elegant space inside a 1614-built,
step-gabled red-brick townhouse.
Exquisite dishes served on hand-
crafted porcelain might include
lobster stuffed with North Sea
crab with vintage Gouda foam or
Texel lamb crown with asparagus
mousse and cinnamon jus (set
menus only on weekends). Book
ahead and dress for the occasion.
(📞020-624 65 89; www.desilveren

spiegel.com; Kattengat 4-6; mains
€28-36.50, 4-/5-/7-/8-course menus
€54.50/75.50/86/96.50; 🕑6-9pm
Mon-Sat; 🚊2/11/12/13/17 Nieuwezijds Kolk)

De Laatste Kruimel   CAFE €

14 🍴 MAP P42, C8

Opening to a tiny canal-side terrace and decorated with vintage
finds from the Noordermarkt
and wooden pallets upcycled as
furniture, the 'Last Crumb' has
glass display cases filled with
pies, quiches, breads, cakes and
lemon-and-poppy-seed scones.
Grandmothers, children, couples
on dates and just about everyone
else crowd in for sweet treats and
fantastic organic sandwiches.
(📞020-423 04 99; www.delaatste
kruimel.nl; Langebrugsteeg 4; dishes

Fo Guang Shan He Hua Temple, Chinatown

Amsterdam's Chinatown

Amsterdam's small Chinatown, with a Buddhist temple, **Kuan Yin Shrine** (Fo Guang Shan He Hua Temple; Map p42, E5; www.ibps.nl; Zeedijk 106-118; ⏰noon-5pm Tue-Sat, 10am-5pm Sun; Ⓜ Nieuwmarkt), centres on Zeedijk. Pan-Asian restaurants popular with locals include **Nam Kee** (Map p42, E5; ☏020-624 34 70; www.namkee.nl; Zeedijk 111-113; mains €12.50-23; ⏰11.30am-10.30pm; Ⓜ Nieuwmarkt), serving Cantonese classics; **New King** (Map p42, E5; ☏020-625 21 80; www.newking. nl; Zeedijk 115-117; mains €12-26; ⏰11am-10.30pm; 🖉; Ⓜ Nieuwmarkt) whose signature Chinese dish is its black-bean steamed oysters; and **Bird Snackbar** (Map p42, E4; ☏020-420 62 89; www.thaibird. nl; Zeedijk 77; mains €10-16; ⏰1-10pm Mon-Wed, to 10.30pm Thu-Sun; 🚊2/4/11/12/13/14/17/24/26 Centraal Station), where cooks turn out Thai favourites loaded with lemongrass, fish sauce or chilli.

€3-10.50; ⏰8am-8pm Mon-Sat, from 9am Sun; Ⓜ Rokin, 🚊4/14/24 Rokin)

Rob Wigboldus Vishandel
SANDWICHES €

15 ❌ MAP P42, C4

A wee three-table oasis in a narrow alleyway just off the touristy Damrak, this fish shop serves excellent herring sandwiches on a choice of white or brown rolls. Other sandwich fillings include smoked eel, Dutch prawns and fried whitefish. (Zoutsteeg 6; sandwiches €3-6.50; ⏰9am-5pm Tue-Sat; 🚊4/14/24 Dam)

Tomaz
DUTCH €€

16 ❌ MAP P42, B7

Charming little Tomaz hides near the Begijnhof and is a fine spot for a light lunch or an informal dinner. Staples include a daily *stamppot* (potato mashed with other vegetables), veal croquettes,

IJsselmeer mussels and Dutch sausages. A vegetarian special is always available. Linger for a while over a game of chess. (☏020-320 64 89; www.tomaz.nl; Begijnensteeg 6-8; mains lunch €8-17, dinner €15-32; ⏰noon-10pm; 🚊2/11/12 Spui)

Drinking

In 't Aepjen
BROWN CAFE

17 🍺 MAP P42, E3

Candles burn even during the day in this 15th-century building – one of two remaining wooden buildings in the city – which has been a tavern since 1519. In the 16th and 17th centuries it was an inn for sailors from the Far East, who often brought *aapjes* (monkeys) to trade for lodging. Vintage jazz on the stereo enhances the time-warp feel. (Zeedijk 1; ⏰noon-1am Mon-Thu, to 3am Fri & Sat; 🚊2/4/11/12/13/14/17/24/26 Centraal Station)

Amsterdam's Coffeeshops

In Amsterdam, *café* (pub) culture should not be mistaken for coffeeshop (marijuana-smoking cafe) culture.

Cannabis is not technically legal in the Netherlands, yet it is widely tolerated. The possession and purchase of 5g of 'soft drugs' (ie marijuana, hashish, space cakes and mushroom-based truffles) is allowed, and users typically aren't prosecuted for smoking or carrying this amount. Coffeeshops are therefore actually conducting an illegal business – but again, this is tolerated to an extent.

Products for Sale

The Netherlands has high-grade home produce, so-called *nederwiet*. It's a particularly strong product – the most potent varieties contain 15% tetrahydrocannabinol (THC), the active substance that gets people high (since 2011, anything above 15% is classified as a hard drug and therefore illegal). Newbies to smoking pot and hash should especially exercise caution.

Space cakes and cookies (baked goods made with hash or marijuana) are also sold in coffeeshops. Most shops offer rolling papers, pipes or bongs to use; you can also buy ready-made joints.

Dos & Don'ts

Do ask coffeeshop staff for the menu of products on offer, and advice on what and how to consume (and heed it). Don't ask for hard (illegal) drugs. Don't drink alcohol – it's illegal in coffeeshops. Don't smoke tobacco, whether mixed with marijuana or on its own – it is forbidden in accordance with Dutch law.

Tales & Spirits
COCKTAIL BAR

18 🕐 MAP P42, B3

Chandeliers glitter beneath wooden beams at Tales & Spirits, which creates its own house infusions, syrups and vinegar-based shrubs. Cocktails such as Any Port in a Storm (Porter's gin, Sailor Jerry spiced rum, sherbet and jalapeño bitters) and the Van Gogh–inspired Drop of Art (with *oude jenever* and absinthe) are

served in vintage and one-of-a-kind glasses. (www.talesandspirits. com; Lijnbaanssteeg 5-7; 🕐5.30pm-1am Tue-Thu & Sun, to 3am Fri & Sat; 🚊2/11/12/13/17 Nieuwezijds Kolk)

Cut Throat
BAR

19 🕐 MAP P42, D4

Beneath 1930s arched brick ceilings, Cut Throat ingeniously combines a men's barbering service (book ahead) with a happening bar

serving international craft beers, cocktails including infused G&Ts (such as blueberry and thyme or mandarin and rosemary), 'spiked' milkshakes and coffee from Amsterdam roastery De Wasserette. Brunch stretches to 4pm daily; all-day dishes span fried chicken and waffles to burgers. (🖉 06 2534 3769; www.cutthroatbarber.nl; Beursplein 5; ⏰ bar noon-11pm Mon-Thu, 11am-2am Fri, 10am-2pm Sat, noon-7pm Sun, barber to 8pm Mon-Fri, to 6pm Sat & Sun; 🛜; 🚊 4/14/24 Dam)

Café de Dokter

BROWN CAFE

20 🚇 MAP P42, B7

Candles flicker on the tables, old jazz records play in the background, and chandeliers and a birdcage hang from the ceiling at atmospheric de Dokter, which at 18 sq metres is allegedly Amsterdam's smallest pub. Whiskeys and smoked beef sausage are specialities. A surgeon opened it in 1798, hence the name. The sixth generation of his family still runs it. (Rozenboomsteeg 4; ⏰ 4pm-1am Wed-Sat; 🚊 2/11/12 Spui)

Brouwerij De Prael

BREWERY

21 🚇 MAP P42, E4

Sample organic beers (Scotch ale, IPA, barley wine and many more varieties) from the socially minded **De Prael brewery** (🖉 020-408 44 70; Oudezijds Voorburgwal 30; tour with 1/4 beers €8.50/17.50; ⏰ tours hourly 1-6pm Mon-Fri, 1-5pm Sat, 2-5pm Sun; 🚊 2/4/11/12/13/14/17/24/26 Centraal Station), known for employing

people with a history of mental illness. Its multilevel taproom has comfy couches and big wooden tables strewn about. There's often live music. A four-beer tasting flight costs €10. (www.deprael.nl; Oudezijds Armsteeg 26; ⏰ noon-midnight Mon-Wed, to 1am Thu-Sat, to 11pm Sun; 🛜; 🚊 2/4/11/12/13/14/17/24/26 Centraal Station)

Hoppe

BROWN CAFE

22 🚇 MAP P42, A8

An Amsterdam institution, Hoppe has been filling glasses since 1670. Barflies and raconteurs toss back brews amid the ancient wood panelling of the *bruin café* (traditional Dutch pub) at No 18 and the more modern, early-20th-century pub at No 20. In all but the iciest weather, the energetic crowd spills out from the dark interior and onto the Spui. (www.cafehoppe.com; Spui 18-20; ⏰ 8am-1am Sun-Thu, to 2am Fri & Sat; 🚊 2/11/12 Spui)

VOC Café

BROWN CAFE

23 🚇 MAP P42, F3

Inside the landmark 15th-century **Schreierstoren** (www.schreierstoren.nl; Prins Hendrikkade 95; 🚊 2/4/11/12/13/14/17/24/26 Centraal Station), this atmospheric *café* (pub) has a historical interior with hefty timber beams and a canal-side terrace. *Jenevers* (Dutch gins), liqueurs and local beers are served alongside classic Dutch bar snacks such as meat-filled *bitterballen* (deep-fried meatballs) and cheese croquettes.

Jenever: Dutch Gin

Jenever (ye-*nay*-ver; Dutch gin – also spelt *genever*) is made from juniper berries and is drunk chilled. It arrives in a tulip-shaped shot glass filled to the brim – tradition dictates that you bend over the bar, with your hands behind your back, and take a deep sip. Most people prefer smooth *jonge* (young) *jenever*; *oude* (old) *jenever* has a strong juniper flavour.

Centuries-old tasting houses where you can try *jenever* include **Wynand Fockink** (p41), **Proeflokaal de Ooievaar** (Map p42, E3; www.proeflokaaldeooievaar.nl; St Olofspoort 1; ⏱noon-midnight; 🚊2/4/11/12/13/14/17/24/26 Centraal Station) and **De Drie Fleschjes** (Map p42, B4; www.dedriefleschjes.nl; Gravenstraat 18; ⏱2-8.30pm Mon-Sat, 3-7pm Sun; 🚊2/11/12/13/17 Dam).

If you're arriving by boat you can dock at its pier. (🕿020-428 82 91; www.schreierstoren.nl; Schreierstoren, Prins Hendrikkade 95; ⏱10am-1am Sun-Thu, to 2.30am Fri & Sat; 🚊2/4/11/12/13/14/17/24/26 Centraal Station)

't Mandje   GAY & LESBIAN

24 ⭐ MAP P42, E4

Amsterdam's oldest gay bar opened in 1927, then shut in 1982 when the Zeedijk grew too seedy. But its trinket-covered interior was lovingly dusted every week until it reopened in 2008. Devoted bartenders can tell you about the bar's brassy lesbian founder Bet van Beeren. It's one of the most *gezellig* (cosy, convivial) places in the centre, gay or straight. (www.cafetmandje.amsterdam; Zeedijk 63; ⏱4pm-1am Tue-Thu, 3pm-3am Fri & Sat, 3pm-1am Sun; 🚊2/4/11/12/13/14/17/24/26 Centraal Station)

Entertainment

Bitterzoet   LIVE MUSIC

25 ⭐ MAP P42, C2

Always full, always changing, this venue with a capacity of just 350 people is one of the friendliest places in town, with a diverse crowd. Music (sometimes live, sometimes courtesy of a DJ) can be funk, roots, drum 'n' bass, Latin, Afro-beat, old-school jazz or hip-hop groove. (🕿020-421 23 18; www.bitterzoet.com; Spuistraat 2; ⏱8pm-late; 🚊2/11/12/13/17 Nieuwezijds Kolk)

Tobacco Theater   THEATRE

26 ⭐ MAP P42, C7

A 1900-built tobacco auction house now contains this architecturally designed theatre, which stages dinner-and-cabaret shows in English, Dutch and German, and presents theatre productions

and concerts. In addition to the 300-capacity theatre, it has an experimental art and concept room in the cellar, along with several lounge areas including a cocktail bar overlooking the stage, and an old bank vault. (📞020-242 06 99; www.tobacco.nl; Nes 75-87; 🚇Rokin, 🚊4/14/24 Rokin)

Shopping

X Bank
DESIGN

27 🔒 MAP P42, A5

More than just a concept store showcasing Dutch-designed haute couture and ready-to-wear fashion, furniture, art, gadgets and homewares, the 700-sq-metre X Bank – in a former bank that's now part of the striking W Amsterdam hotel – also hosts exhibitions, workshops,

launches and lectures. Interior displays change every month; check the website for upcoming events. (www.xbank.amsterdam; Spuistraat 172; ⏱10am-8pm Fri-Wed, to 9pm Thu; 🚊2/11/12/13/17 Dam)

Locals
FASHION & ACCESSORIES

28 🔒 MAP P42, A7

Jeweller Suzanne Hof set up this boutique to showcase designs from her own label, Sugarz, but also to provide a platform for small-scale designers from the Netherlands and especially from Amsterdam. Along with men's and women's fashion (T-shirts, jeans, dresses), you'll find scarves, hats, gloves, handbags and homewares (vases, cushions, crockery, paintings and contemporary twists on hand-painted Delftware tiles).

Musician from band BKO Quintet performing at Bitterzoet

(www.localsamsterdam.com; Spuistraat 272; ⏱1-6pm Mon, 11.30am-6pm Tue-Sat, noon-6pm Sun; 🚋2/11/12 Spui)

Mark Raven Grafiek
GIFTS & SOUVENIRS

29 🔒 MAP P42, B4

Artist Mark Raven's distinctive vision of Amsterdam is available on posters, coasters and well-cut T-shirts that make great souvenirs. Prices are impressively reasonable and there's often a sale rack out front. (www.markraven.nl; Nieuwezijds Voorburgwal 174; ⏱10.30am-6pm; 🚋1/2/5/13/14/17 Dam)

Bonbon Boutique
JEWELLERY

30 🔒 MAP P42, B7

A white-on-white space is the backdrop for Amsterdam-designed jewellery (rings, earrings, bracelets, necklaces and pendants) crafted from gold, sterling silver, brass, precious stones and coloured crystal. Jewellery-making workshops in English and Dutch (from €60 for two hours) teach you hammering, bending, cutting and filing techniques on creations you get to keep. (www.bonbonboutique.nl; Rosmarijnsteeg 8; ⏱11am-6pm Mon-Sat, noon-6pm Sun; 🚋2/11/12 Spui)

Mary Go Wild
MUSIC

31 🔒 MAP P42, E4

House and techno are the specialities of this vinyl shop on Zeedijk. DJs often play in-store; it also has its own online radio station, and hosts occasional raves in its basement. It's one of the best sources

Magna Plaza

MANORBIOTIU/SHUTTERSTOCK ©

of information for clubbing events around town. (www.marygowild.nl; Zeedijk 44; ⏲1-7pm Wed & Sun, noon-8pm Thu, noon-7pm Fri & Sat; 🚊2/4/11/12/13/14/17/24/26 Centraal Station)

Hempstory CONCEPT STORE

32 🔒 MAP P42, D6

Everything at this light-filled contemporary boutique is made from hemp: skincare ranges (soaps, moisturisers, and body washes such as hemp and ginseng), insect repellent, homewares (blankets, throws, cushions, botanical prints on hemp paper), men's and women's clothing (shirts, jackets, scarves, hats), and hemp-cord jewellery. Its tiny cafe serves (non-active) hemp tea, hemp-seed cakes and hemp-seed smoothies. (www.hempstory.nl; Oudezijds Achterburgwal 142; ⏲11am-7pm Tue-Wed, Fri-Sat, to 9pm Thu, noon-7pm Sun & Mon; 🚊4/14/24 Dam)

Magna Plaza MALL

33 🔒 MAP P42, B5

This grand 19th-century landmark building, once the main post office, is now home to an upmarket shopping mall with more than 40 boutiques stocking fashion, gifts and jewellery – everything from Mango and Sissy Boy to a cashmere specialist. After browsing, stop for refreshments at its 1100 sq metre food hall, where choices include Amsterdam burger specialist the **Butcher** (www.the-butcher.com;

Art & Book Markets

Save on gallery fees by buying direct from the artists at Amsterdam's weekly **art market** (Map p42, B8; www.artamsterdam-spui.com; Spui; ⏲11am-6pm Sun Mar-Dec; 🚊2/11/12 Spui). Some 60 Dutch and contemporary artists set up on the square. Old tomes, maps and sheet music are the speciality at the daily (bar Sunday) **Oudemanhuispoort Book Market** (Map p42, D7; Oudemanhuispoort; ⏲11am-4pm Mon-Sat; Ⓜ Rokin, 🚊4/14/24 Rokin).

Paleisstraat 14; burgers €6.50-12.50; ⏲11am-1am Sun-Thu, to 3am Fri & Sat; 🚊2/11/12/13/17 Dam). (www.magnaplaza.nl; Nieuwezijds Voorburgwal 182; ⏲10am-10pm; 🚊1/2/5/13/14/17 Dam)

Condomerie het Gulden Vlies ADULT

34 🔒 MAP P42, D5

In the heart of the Red Light District, this brightly lit boutique sells condoms in every imaginable size, colour, flavour and design (horned devils, marijuana leaves, Delftware tiles...), along with lubricants and saucy gifts. Photos aren't allowed inside the shop. (www.condomerie.com; Warmoesstraat 141; ⏲11am-9pm Mon & Wed-Sat, to 6pm Tue, 1-6pm Sun; 🚊4/14/24 Dam)

Walking Tour 🚶

Amsterdam's Splashiest Canals

More canals flow in Amsterdam than in Venice. Get the camera ready, because this walk passes some of the city's most beautiful waterways. For more than four centuries the canals have performed the epic task of keeping Amsterdam above water, since they help help drain the soggy landscape. Today 100km of channels do their duty.

x

Getting There

This walk starts in Nieuwmarkt and winds for 3km along and around the Amstel river, from which Amsterdam takes its name.

🚋 24 Muntplein

Ⓜ Nieuwmarkt

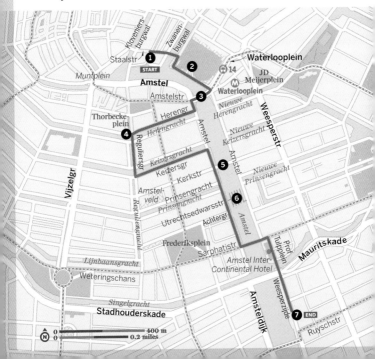

❶ Groenburgwal

Step out onto the white drawbridge that crosses the **Groenburgwal** and look north. Many Amsterdammers swear this is the loveliest canal view of all – a pick backed by Impressionist Claude Monet, who painted it in 1874 as *The Zuiderkerk (South Church) at Amsterdam: Looking up the Groenburgwal.*

❷ Stopera

Head to the **Stopera** building, Amsterdam's combination of city hall and **Muziektheater** (p162). Its terrace is a great place for sitting and watching the boats go by on the Amstel.

❸ Blauwbrug

Cross the river via the 1884 **Blauwbrug** (Blue Bridge; btwn Waterlooplein & Amstelstraat; Ⓜ Waterlooplein, 🚊14 Waterlooplein) (Blue Bridge). Inspired by Paris' Alexander III bridge, it features tall, ornate street lamps topped by the imperial crown of Amsterdam, fish sculptures, and foundations shaped like a medieval ship prow.

❹ Reguliersgracht

Walk along the Herengracht to **Reguliersgracht** (p89), the 'seven bridges' canal. Start with your back to the Thorbeckeplein and the Herengracht flowing directly in front of you. Lean over the bridge

and sigh at the seven humpbacked arches leading down the canal straight ahead.

❺ Magere Brug

Walk along the Keizergracht and turn right towards the wedding-photo-favourite **Magere Brug** (Skinny Bridge; btwn Kerkstraat & Nieuwe Kerkstraat; 🚊4 Prinsengracht) (Skinny Bridge). According to legend, two sisters built it. They lived on opposite sides of the river and wanted an easy way to visit each other. Alas, they only had enough money to construct a narrow bridge.

❻ Amstelsluizen

Continue south to the **Amstelsluizen** (Amstel Locks; 🚊4 Prinsengracht). These impressive locks, dating from 1674, allow the canals to be flushed with fresh water. The sluices on the city's west side are left open as the stagnant water is pumped out to sea.

❼ De Ysbreeker

Cross the river once more; take Prof Tulpplein past the Inter-Continental hotel to **De Ysbreeker** (p143). The building used to be an inn for the tough guys who broke ice on the Amstel so boats could pass. Grab a seat on the enormous waterfront terrace to see what's gliding by these days.

Explore

Jordaan & the Western Canal Ring

If Amsterdam's neighbourhoods held a 'best personality' contest, the Jordaan would surely win. Its intimacy is contagious, with jovial bar singalongs, candlelit bruin cafés (traditional Dutch pubs) and flower-box-adorned eateries spilling out onto narrow streets. The Western Canal Ring's waterways flow next door. Grand old buildings and oddball speciality shops line the glinting waterways.

The Short List

○ **Anne Frank Huis (p60)** *Contemplating the brave life and tragic death of Anne Frank where she and her family hid from the Nazis.*

○ **Negen Straatjes (p63)** *Browsing the speciality shops along these 'nine streets' criss-crossed by canals.*

○ **Westerkerk (p66)** *Scaling the bell tower and catching a carillon recital.*

○ **Reypenaer Cheese Tasting (p70)** *Learning to distinguish an aged Gouda from a young boerenkaas (farmer's cheese).*

○ **De Twee Zwaantjes (p74)** *Spending the evening in the Jordaan's bruin cafés.*

Getting There & Around

🚊 Trams 3, 5, 7, 17 and 19 skirt the neighbourhood's western edge; trams 13 and 17 go through its centre.

🚌 Buses 18, 21, 22 and 48 provide the quickest access from Centraal Station to the neighbourhood's north and west, and the Western Islands.

🚗 Don't try to drive through the Jordaan's narrow streets.

Neighbourhood Map on p64

Negen Straatjes (p63) DENNIS VAN DE WATER/SHUTTERSTOCK ©

Top Experience 📷

Remember the Past at Anne Frank Huis

It is one of the 20th century's most compelling stories: a young Jewish girl forced into hiding with her family and their friends to escape deportation by the Nazis. The house they used as a hideaway should be a highlight of any visit to Amsterdam; indeed, it attracts some 1¼ million visitors a year.

◎ MAP P64, D5

📞 020-556 71 05

www.annefrank.org

Prinsengracht 263-267

adult/child €10.50/5.50

�途 9am-10pm Apr-Oct, 9am-7pm Sun-Fri, to 10pm Sat Nov-Mar

🚊 13/17 Westermarkt

The Residents

The Franks moved into the upper floors of the specially prepared rear of the building, along with another couple, the Van Pels (called the Van Daans in Anne's diary), and their son, Peter. Four months later Fritz Pfeffer (called Mr Dussel in the diary) joined the household. Here they survived until they were betrayed to the Gestapo in August 1944.

Offices & Warehouse

The building originally held Otto Frank's pectin (a substance used in jelly-making) business. On the lower floors you'll see the former offices of Victor Kugler, Otto's business partner; and the desks of Miep Gies, Bep Voskuijl and Jo Kleiman, all of whom worked in the office and provided food, clothing and other goods for the household. The museum shows multilingual news reels of WWII footage narrated using segments of Anne's diary.

Secret Annexe

The upper floors in the Achterhuis (rear house) contain the Secret Annexe, where the living quarters have been preserved in powerful austerity. As you enter Anne's small bedroom, you can still see the remnants of a young girl's dreams; the photos of Hollywood stars and postcards of the Dutch royal family she pasted on the wall.

The Diary

More haunting exhibits and videos await after you return to the front house – including Anne's red-plaid diary itself, sitting alone in its glass case. Watch the video of Anne's old schoolmate Hanneli Goslar, who describes encountering Anne at Bergen-Belsen. Read heartbreaking letters from Otto, the only Secret Annexe occupant to survive the concentration camps.

★ Top Tips

o In spring and summer, take advantage of the house's extended evening hours. Go for an early dinner at one of the many excellent nearby cafes, and then spend the rest of the evening hours in Amsterdam's most moving sight – with fewer crowds and plenty of time to contemplate this remarkable Dutch girl's life and legacy.

o Interior photography is not permitted.

o There are many stairs; only the modern museum is accessible for wheelchairs.

o The cafe and shop are only accessible to ticket holders.

✖ Take a Break

Bistro Bij Ons (p70) serves classic Dutch dishes in charming surrounds.

For a quick, filling snack, head to famous frites (fries) stand Wil Graanstra Friteshuis (p71).

Jordaan & the Western Canal Ring Anne Frank Huis

Walking Tour 🥾

Shopping the Jordaan & Western Canal Ring

These are Amsterdam's prime neighbourhoods for stumbling upon offbeat little shops selling items you'd find nowhere else. Velvet ribbons? Herb-spiced Gouda? Vintage jewellery? They're all here amid the Western Canals' quirky stores and the Jordaan's eclectic boutiques and markets. Everything is squashed into a grid of tiny lanes – a perfect place for an afternoon stroll.

Walk Facts

Start Antiekcentrum Amsterdam

End De Kat in de Wijngaert

Length 3.2km; two hours

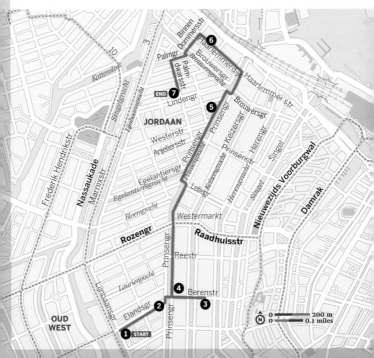

❶ Antiqueing at Antiekcentrum

Anyone who likes peculiar old stuff might enter **Antiekcentrum Amsterdam** (Amsterdam Antique Centre; www.antiekcentrumamsterdam.nl; Elandsgracht 109; ⏲11am-6pm Mon & Wed-Fri, to 5pm Sat & Sun; 🚊5/7/17/19 Elandsgracht), a knick-knack mini-mall, and never come out.

❷ Tunes at Johnny Jordaanplein

The small square **Johnny Jordaanplein** (cnr Prinsengracht & Elandsgracht; 🚊13/17 Westermarkt) is dedicated to the local hero and musician who sang the romantic music known as *levenslied* (tears-in-your-beer-style ballads).

❸ Wander the Negen Straatjes

The **Negen Straatjes** (Nine Streets; www.de9straatjes.nl; 🚊2/11/12 Spui) comprise a tic-tac-toe board of wee shops dealing in fashion (both vintage and emerging new designers), housewares and specialities. It's bounded by Reestraat, Hartenstraat and Gasthuismolensteeg to the north and Runstraat, Huidenstraat and Wijde Heisteeg to the south.

❹ Dutch Pancakes

At **Pancakes!** (📞020-528 97 97; www.pancakes.amsterdam; Berenstraat 38; mains €6-13; ⏲8am-6pm; 🛜♿🚻; 🚊13/17 Westermarkt) you can order this signature Dutch favourite in both savoury and sweet versions or a combination of both, such as grated Dutch cheese and Jonagold apples.

❺ Rummage the Noordermarkt

The **Noordermarkt** (Northern Market; www.jordaanmarkten.nl; Noordermarkt; ⏲flea market 9am-1pm Mon, farmers market 9am-3pm Sat; 🚊3/5 Marnixplein) surrounds the Noorderkerk and hosts two bazaars. On Monday mornings it's a trove of secondhand clothing and assorted antique trinkets. On Saturdays, most of the clothing stalls are replaced by produce from around Amsterdam.

❻ Get Hip on Haarlemmerdijk

The street **Haarlemmerdijk** buzzes with stylish shops and lots of places to snack or unwind over a drink.

❼ Relax at De Kat in de Wijngaert

De Kat in de Wijngaert (www.dekatindewijngaert.nl; Lindengracht 160; ⏲10am-1am Sun-Thu, to 3am Fri, 9am-3am Sat; 🚊3 Marnixplein) is the kind of *bruin café* where you can easily find yourself settling in for a while.

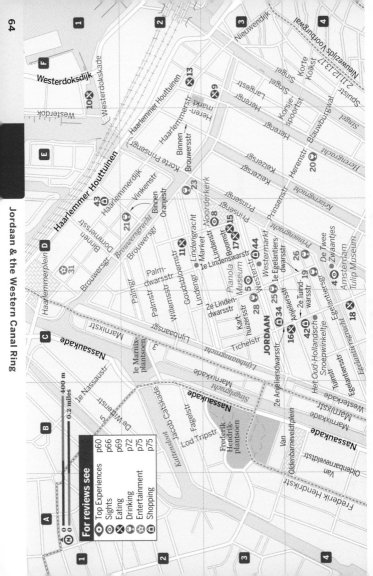

Jordaan & the Western Canal Ring

Westerdoksdijk

Haarlemmer Houttuinen

JORDAAN

For reviews see
Top Experiences p60
Sights p66
Eating p69
Drinking p72
Entertainment p75
Shopping p75

400 m
0.2 miles

Nassaukade

Frederik
Hendrik-
plantsoen

Amsterdam
Tulip Museum

Westermarkt

Pianola
Museum

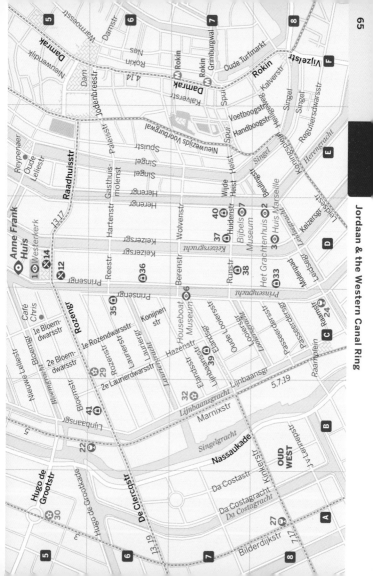

Sights

Westerkerk CHURCH

1 ⊙ MAP P64, D5

The main gathering place for Amsterdam's Dutch Reformed community, this church was built for rich Protestants to a 1620 design by Hendrick de Keyser. The nave is the largest in the Netherlands and is covered by a wooden barrel vault. The huge main organ dates from 1686, with panels decorated with instruments and biblical scenes. Rembrandt (1606–69), who died bankrupt at nearby Rozengracht, was buried in a pauper's grave somewhere in the church. Its **bell tower** (☏020-689 25 65; www.westertorenamsterdam. nl; Prinsengracht 281; tours €9; ⏰9am-8pm Mon-Sat Apr-Sep, 9am-5.30pm Oct; ◧13/17 Westermarkt) can be climbed. (Western Church; ☏020-624 77 66; www.westerkerk.nl; Prinsengracht 281; ⏰10am-3pm Mon-Sat early May-Oct, 10am-3pm Mon-Fri Nov-early May; ◧13/17 Westermarkt)

Het Grachtenhuis MUSEUM

2 ⊙ MAP P64, D8

Learn about the remarkable feats of engineering behind the Canal Ring through this museum's holograms, videos, models, cartoons, scale model of Amsterdam and other innovative exhibits, which explain how the canals and the houses that line them were built. Unlike at most Amsterdam museums, you can't simply wander through: small groups go in together to experience the multimedia exhibits. It takes about 45 minutes, and you'll come out knowing why Amsterdam's houses tilt. Admission includes an audioguide. (Canal House; ☏020-421 16 56; www.hetgrachtenhuis.nl; Herengracht 386; adult/child €15/7.50; ⏰10am-5pm Tue-Sun; ◧2/11/12 Koningsplein)

Huis Marseille MUSEUM

3 ⊙ MAP P64, D8

Large-scale temporary exhibitions from its own collection are staged at this well-curated photography museum, which also hosts travelling shows. Themes might include portraiture, nature or regional photography. Exhibitions are spread out over several floors and in a summer house behind the main house. French merchant Isaac Focquier built Huis Marseille in 1665, installing a map of the French port Marseille on the facade, and the original structure has remained largely intact. (☏020-531 89 89; www.huismarseille. nl; Keizersgracht 401; adult/child €9/free; ⏰11am-6pm Tue-Sun; ◧2/11/12 Keizersgracht)

Amsterdam Tulip Museum MUSEUM

4 ⊙ MAP P64, D4

Allow around half an hour at this diminutive museum, which offers an overview of the history of the country's favourite bloom. Through exhibits, timelines and

Amsterdam's Canals

Far from being simply decorative or picturesque, or even waterways for transport, the city's canals were crucial to drain and reclaim the waterlogged land. They solved Amsterdam's essential problem: keeping the land and sea separate.

Core Canals

Amsterdam's core canals include the singular **Singel**, originally a moat that defended Amsterdam's outer limits.

Beyond it is the **Herengracht** (Gentlemen's Canal), where Amsterdam's wealthiest residents built their mansions, particularly around the Golden Bend.

Almost as swanky was the **Keizersgracht** (Emperor's Canal), a nod to Holy Roman Emperor Maximilian I.

The **Prinsengracht** – named after William the Silent, Prince of Orange and the first Dutch royal – had smaller residences and warehouses. It acted as a barrier against the working-class Jordaan beyond.

Radial Canals

Cutting across the core canals like spokes on a bicycle wheel are the radial canals.

The **Brouwersgracht** (Brewers Canal) is one of Amsterdam's most beautiful waterways. It takes its name from the many breweries that lined the banks in the 16th and 17th centuries.

The **Leidsegracht** was named after the city of Leiden, to which it was the main water route.

Peaceful **Reguliersgracht** was named after an order of monks whose monastery was located nearby.

two short films (in English), you'll learn how Ottoman merchants encountered the flowers in the Himalayan steppes and began commercial production in Turkey, how fortunes were made and lost during Dutch 'Tulipmania' in the 17th century, and how bulbs were used as food during WWII. You'll also discover present-day growing and harvesting techniques.

(020-421 00 95; www.amsterdam tulipmuseum.com; Prinsengracht 116; adult/child €5/3; 10am-6pm; 13/17 Westermarkt)

Pianola Museum
MUSEUM

5 MAP P64, D3

This is a very special place, crammed with pianolas from the early 1900s. The museum has

around 50, although only a dozen are on display at any given time, as well as some 30,000 music rolls and a player pipe organ. The curator gives an hour-long guided tour and music demonstrations with great zest. Regular concerts are held on the player pianos, featuring anything from Mozart to Fats Waller and rare classical or jazz tunes composed specially for the instrument. (☎020-627 96 24; www. pianola.nl; Westerstraat 106; museum adult/child €9/5, concert tickets from €12.50; ⏱11am-5pm Fri & Sat, to 4pm Sun year-round, concerts Sep-Jun; 🚃3/5 Marnixplein)

Houseboat Museum   MUSEUM

6 ◉ MAP P64, C7

This quirky museum, a 23m-long sailing barge from 1914, offers a good sense of how *gezellig* (cosy) life can be on the water. The actual displays are minimal, but you can watch a presentation on houseboats (some pretty and some ghastly) and inspect the sleeping, living, cooking and dining quarters with all the mod cons. Cash only. (☎020-427 07 50; www.houseboat museum.nl; Prinsengracht 296k; adult/child €4.50/3.50; ⏱10am-5pm daily Jul & Aug, Tue-Sun Sep-Jun; 🚃13/17 Westermarkt)

Bijbels Museum   MUSEUM

7 ◉ MAP P64, D7

A scale model of the Jewish Tabernacle described in Exodus – built by dedicated minister Leendert Schouten and drawing thousands of visitors even before it was completed in 1851 – is the star attraction at this bible museum. Inside a 1622 canal house, the museum has an extraordinary collection of bibles, including the Netherlands' oldest, a 1477-printed Delft Bible, and a 1st edition of the 1637 Dutch authorised version. Trees and plants mentioned in the Good Book feature in the garden. (Bible Museum; ☎020-624 24 36; www.bijbelsmuseum.nl; Herengracht 366-368; adult/child €12.50/free; ⏱10am-5pm; 🚃2/11/12 Spui)

Noorderkerk   CHURCH

8 ◉ MAP P64, D3

Near the Prinsengracht's northern end, this imposing Calvinist church was completed in 1623 for the 'common' people in the Jordaan. (The upper classes attended the Westerkerk further south.) It was built in the shape of a broad Greek cross (four arms of equal length) around a central pulpit, giving the entire congregation unimpeded access. Hendrick de Keyser's design, unusual at the time, would become common for Protestant churches throughout the country. It hosts the well-regarded Saturday-afternoon **Noorderkerk-concerten** (www.noorderkerk concerten.nl; Noorderkerk, Noordermarkt 44; tickets from €16.50; ⏱2pm Sat; 🚃3/5 Marnixplein) concert series. (Northern Church; www. noorderkerk.org; Noordermarkt 48; ⏱10.30am-12.30pm Mon, 11am-1pm Sat; 🚃3/5 Marnixplein)

Cheese tasting at Reypenaer (p70)

Eating

Eating

De Belhamel

EUROPEAN €€

 9 MAP P64, F3

In warm weather the canal-side tables here at the head of the Herengracht are enchanting, and the richly wallpapered art nouveau interior set over two levels provides the perfect backdrop for exquisitely presented dishes such as poached sole with wild-spinach bisque, veal sweetbreads with polenta and spring onion jus, or a half lobster with velvety truffle mayonnaise. (☎020-622 10 95; www.belhamel.nl; Brouwersgracht 60; mains €24-26, 3-/4-course menus €38/48; ☉noon-4pm & 5.30-10pm; 🚊18/21/22 Buiten Brouwersstraat)

Wolf Atelier

GASTRONOMY €€

10 MAP P64, F1

Atop a 1920 railway swing bridge, a glass box with pivoting windows is the showcase for experimental chef Michael Wolf's wild flavour combinations: hazelnut-crusted foie gras, langoustine tartare with hollandaise, oxtail velouté with daikon, and blueberry crème brûlée with blackberry Chantilly cream and raspberry dust. The 360-degree views are magical at night; diners can linger for a drink until 1am. (☎020-344 64 28; www.wolfatelier.nl; Westerdoksplein 20; mains €25, 4-/5-/15-course menus €46/52/78; ☉noon-5pm & 6-10pm Mon-Sat; 🚊18/21/22 Buiten Brouwersstraat)

Cheese Tasting

Here's your chance to become a *kaas* (cheese) connoisseur: century-old Dutch cheesemaker **Reypenaer** (Map p64, E5; 020-320 63 33; www.reypenaercheese.com; Singel 182; tastings from €17.50; tastings by reservation; 2/11/12/13/17 Dam) offers tastings in a rustic classroom beneath its shop. The hour-long session includes six cheeses – four cow's milk, two goat's milk – from young to old, with wine and port pairings. Expert staff members guide you through them, helping you appreciate the cheeses' look, aroma and taste.

Daalder GASTRONOMY €€€

11 MAP P64, D2

An unassuming black facade conceals a spectacular interior with terrazzo floors, a marble bar and designer lighting. Daalder serves unforgettable contemporary Dutch cuisine. Surprise menus might span a lobster meringue amuse-bouche with red seaweed foam, to scallop carpaccio with coriander-infused gin gel, lamb neck with black-garlic mousse and caramel-centred *stroopwafel* cake with *speculaas* (spiced biscuit) crumb and white-pepper ice cream. (020-624 88 64; www.daalderamsterdam.nl; Lindengracht 90; 3-/4-course lunch menu €37.50/45, 5-/7-course dinner menus €69/89; 6.30-9.30pm Thu,

noon-2pm & 6.30-9.30pm Fri-Mon; 3 Nieuwe Willemsstraat)

Bistro Bij Ons DUTCH €€

12 MAP P64, D5

If you're not in town visiting your Dutch *oma* (grandma), try the honest-to-goodness cooking at this charming retro bistro instead. Classics include *stamppot* (potatoes mashed with another vegetable) with sausage, *raasdonders* (split peas with bacon, onion and pickles) and *poffertjes* (small pancakes with butter and powdered sugar). House-made liqueurs include plum and *drop* (liquorice) varieties. (020-627 90 16; www.bistrobijons.nl; Prinsengracht 287; mains €12.50-21.50; 11am-10pm Tue-Sun; 13/17 Westermarkt)

Vinnies Deli CAFE €

13 MAP P64, F2

Only organic, locally sourced produce is used in Vinnes' extensive all-day breakfasts, gourmet sandwiches, lush salads, creative cakes and hot specials such as kale-and-mushroom frittata or roasted miso-marinated aubergine. Coffee is from Amsterdam roastery Bocca. Vegan options abound. If you're imagining the cafe's designer furniture in your lounge room, you're in luck: all the pieces are for sale. (www.vinnieshomepage.com; Haarlemmerstraat 46; mains €6-14.50; 7.30am-5pm Mon-Fri, 9am-5pm Sat, 9.30am-5pm Sun; 2/4/11/12/13/14/17/24/26 Centraal Station)

Wil Graanstra Friteshuis
FAST FOOD €

14 ⊗ MAP P64, D5

Legions of Amsterdammers swear by the crispy chips at Wil Graanstra Friteshuis. The family-run business has been frying on the square by the Westerkerk since 1956. Most locals top their cones with mayonnaise, though *oorlog* (a peanut sauce–mayo combo), curry sauce and piccalilli (relish) rock the taste buds too. Cash only. (Westermarkt 11; frites €3-4.50, sauce €0.30-0.50; ⏰noon-7pm Mon-Sat; 🚊13/17 Westermarkt)

Winkel
CAFE €

15 ⊗ MAP P64, D3

This sprawling, indoor-outdoor space is great for people-watching, popular for breakfast (organic muesli, omelettes), coffees and small meals such as wild-boar stew with sauerkraut and cranberry sauce. Its tall, cakey apple pie, served with clouds of whipped cream, hits it out of the park. On market days (Monday and Saturday) there's almost always a queue out the door. (www.winkel43.nl; Noordermarkt 43; dishes €4-9; ⏰kitchen 7am-10pm Mon & Sat, 8am-10pm Tue-Fri, 10am-10pm Sun, bar to 1am Sun-Thu, to 3am Fri & Sat; 📶; 🚊3/5 Marnixplein)

Trattoria di Donna Sofia
ITALIAN €€

16 ⊗ MAP P64, C4

With rustic decor and white-clothed tables, Donna Sofia – named for the owner's grandmother – has a daily-changing blackboard menu of Neapolitan dishes chalked in Italian. Pastas are made in-house and risottos are a speciality; fresh herbs enhance the flavours of the fish, meat and vegetarian dishes. All-Italian vintages feature on the small but well-chosen wine list. (☎020-623 41 04; www.trattoriadidonnasofia.com; Anjeliersstraat 300; mains €14-29.50; ⏰5-11pm; 🚊3/5 Marnixplein)

Boca's
TAPAS €€

17 ⊗ MAP P64, D3

Fronted by a red awning and white-timber facade, this hip little bar is the perfect place for a drink accompanied by bar snacks. Try the mini lasagnes, burgers, bruschetta and steak tartar, or bigger selections on wooden boards: cheese platters, veggie platters, seafood platters, meat platters, sweet platters. If you can't decide, go for Boca's combination platter. (☎020-820 37 27; www.bar-bocas.nl; Westerstraat 30; bar snacks €3.50-7, platters €21-58.50; ⏰kitchen 9am-9pm Mon & Sat, 10am-9pm Tue-Fri, 11am-9pm Sun, bar to 1am Sun-Thu, to 3am Fri & Sat; 📶; 🚊3/5 Marnixplein)

De Reiger
DUTCH €€

18 ⊗ MAP P64, C4

Assiduously local and very atmospheric, this corner *café* (pub) – one of the Jordaan's oldest, with high beamed ceilings and art nouveau and art deco fittings – has a quiet front bar and a noisy, more

ROCKERSTOCKER/SHUTTERSTOCK ©

't Smalle

spacious dining section at the back serving a short but stellar menu (venison and stewed pear with honey-cinnamon sauce, for instance). No reservations or credit cards. (www.dereigeramsterdam.nl; Nieuwe Leliestraat 34; mains €18.50-24.50; ⏱5-9.30pm Tue-Fri, noon-4pm & 6-10.30pm Sat, 4-10.30pm Sun, bar to 11.30pm Tue-Fri, to 10.30pm Sat & Sun; 🚊13/17 Westermarkt)

Drinking

't Smalle   BROWN CAFE

19 🚇 MAP P64, D4

Dating back to 1786 as a *jenever* (Dutch gin) distillery and tasting house, and restored during the 1970s with antique porcelain beer pumps and lead-framed windows, this locals' favourite is one of

Amsterdam's most charming *bruin cafés*. Dock your boat right by the pretty stone terrace, which is wonderfully convivial by day and impossibly romantic at night. (Egelantiersgracht 12; ⏱10am-1am Sun-Thu, to 2am Fri & Sat; 🚊13/17 Westermarkt)

't Arendsnest   BROWN CAFE

20 🚇 MAP P64, E4

This gorgeous restyled *bruin café*, with glowing copper *jenever* (Dutch gin) boilers behind the bar, only serves Dutch beer – but with more than 100 varieties (many from small breweries), including 52 rotating on tap, you'll need to move here to try them all. It also has more than 40 gins, ciders, whiskies and liqueurs, all of which are Dutch too. (www.arendsnest.nl; Herengracht 90;

⏱noon-midnight Sun-Thu, to 2am Fri & Sat; 🚊2/11/12/13/17 Nieuwezijds Kolk)

Vesper Bar
COCKTAIL BAR

21 🚇 MAP P64, D2

This luxe bar's location on a low-key stretch of Jordaanian shops and businesses gives it a certain mystique. Its martinis will coax out your inner James Bond – or Vesper Lynd (the lead female character in *Casino Royale*). Other cocktails include Q's Old Fashioned (rye whiskey, cherry-leaf syrup, bitters and cracked coffee beans). (www.vesperbar.nl; Vinkenstraat 57; ⏱6pm-1am Tue-Thu, 5pm-3am Fri & Sat; 🛜; 🚊18/21/22 Buiten Oranjestraat)

Cafe Soundgarden
BAR

22 🚇 MAP P64, B6

In this grungy all-ages dive bar, the 'Old Masters' are the Ramones and Black Sabbath. Somehow a handful of pool tables, 1980s and '90s pinball machines, unkempt DJs and lovably surly bartenders add up to an ineffable magic. Bands occasionally make an appearance, and the waterfront terrace scene is more like an impromptu party in someone's backyard. (www.cafesoundgarden.nl; Marnixstraat 164-166; ⏱1pm-1am Mon-Thu, to 3am Fri, 3pm-3am Sat, to 1am Sun; 🛜; 🚊5/13/17/19 Marnixstraat)

Café Papeneiland
BROWN CAFE

23 🚇 MAP P64, E2

With Delft Blue tiles and a central stove, this *bruin café* is a 1642

Gezelligheid: A Dutch Quality

This particularly Dutch quality, which is most widely found in old brown cafes, is one of the best reasons to visit Amsterdam. It's variously translated as 'snug', 'friendly', 'cosy', 'informal' and 'convivial', but *gezelligheid* – the state of being *gezellig* – is more elemental. You'll feel this all-is-right-with-the-world vibe in many places and situations, often while nursing a brew with friends during *borrel* (an informal gathering over drinks). And nearly any low-lit, welcoming establishment qualifies.

gem. The name, 'Papists' Island', goes back to the Reformation, when there was a clandestine Catholic church on the canal's northern side. Papeneiland was reached via a secret tunnel from the top of the stairs – ask bar staff to show you the entrance. (Prinsengracht 2; ⏱10am-1am Sun-Thu, to 3am Fri & Sat; 🚊3/5 Marnixplein)

Café Pieper
BROWN CAFE

24 🚇 MAP P64, C8

Small, unassuming and unmistakably old (1665), Café Pieper features stained-glass windows, antique beer mugs hanging from the bar and a working Belgian beer pump (1875). Sip an Amsterdam-brewed Brouwerij 't

Drink Like a Jordaanian

There's a certain hard-drinking, hard-living spirit left over from the Jordaan's working-class days, when the neighbourhood burst with 80,000 residents (compared to today's 20,000) and *bruin cafés* functioned as a refuge from the slings and arrows of workaday life. Local bastions that are still going strong include **De Twee Zwaantjes** (Map p64, D4; 📞020-625 27 29; www.cafedetweezwaantjes.nl; Prinsengracht 114; ⊙3pm-1am Sun-Thu, noon-3am Fri & Sat; 🚊13/17 Westermarkt) – at its hilarious best on Wednesday nights, when patrons and staff belt out classic Dutch tunes, and Thursday nights, when cabaret meets karaoke – and the Jordaan's oldest, **Café Chris** (Map p64, C5; www.cafechris.nl; Bloemstraat 42; ⊙3pm-1am Mon-Thu, to 2am Fri & Sat, to 9pm Sun; 🚊13/17 Westermarkt).

IJ beer or a terrific cappuccino as you marvel at the claustrophobia of the low-ceilinged bar (people were shorter back in the 17th century – even the Dutch it seems). (www.facebook.com/CafePieper; Prinsengracht 424; ⊙4pm-midnight Mon & Tue, noon-1am Wed & Thu, noon-2am Fri & Sat, 1pm-midnight Sun; 🚊2/12 Prinsengracht)

Drupa
COFFEE

25 🚇 MAP P64, D3

'Farm to cup' coffee here focuses on Colombian beans, which Drupa roasts, grinds and brews utilising methods including V60, Chemex and Kyoto-style cold-brew towers. The white-painted interior has a handful of seats at tiny tables, or you can pick up a coffee (and bags of beans) to go. (www.drupacoffee.com; 1e Anjeliersdwarsstraat 16a; ⊙9am-5.30pm Tue-Fri, 10am-5.30pm Sat & Sun; 🛜; 🚊3/5 Marnixplein)

Café P 96
BROWN CAFE

26 🚇 MAP P64, D4

If you don't want the night to end, P 96 is an amiable hang-out. When most other *cafés* (pubs) in the Jordaan shut down for the night, this is where everyone ends up, rehashing their evening and striking up conversations with strangers. In summertime head to the terrace across the street aboard a houseboat. (www.p96.nl; Prinsengracht 96; ⊙11am-3am Sun-Thu, to 4am Fri & Sat; 🛜; 🚊13/17 Westermarkt)

De Trut
GAY & LESBIAN

27 🚇 MAP P64, A8

In the basement of a former squat, this Sunday-night club is a gay and lesbian institution. It's run by volunteers and comes with an attitude; arrive well before 11pm (the space is fairly small). No cameras are allowed inside; phones must

be turned off. (www.trutfonds.nl; Bilderdijkstraat 165e; ⏰10pm-4am Sun; 🚊3/7/13/19 Bilderdijkstraat/Kinkerstraat)

Café 't Monumentje BROWN CAFE

28 🚇 MAP P64, C3

This slightly scruffy yet lovable *café* (pub) is always heaving with local barflies. It's a fun spot for a beer and a snack after shopping at the Westermarkt. Singalongs take place on the first Monday of the month; it also hosts occasional live music. (www.monumentje.nl; Westerstraat 120; ⏰8.30am-1am Mon-Thu, to 3am Fri, 9am-3am Sat, 11am-1am Sun; 🚊3/5 Marnixplein)

Entertainment

Boom Chicago COMEDY

29 ⭐ MAP P64, C6

Boom Chicago stages seriously funny improv-style comedy shows in English that make fun of Dutch culture, American culture and everything that gets in the crosshairs. Edgier shows happen in the smaller upstairs theatre. The on-site bar helps fuel the festivities with buckets of ice and beer. (☎020-217 04 00; www.boomchicago.nl; Rozengracht 117; 📶; 🚊5/13/17/19 Marnixstraat/Rozengracht)

De Nieuwe Anita ARTS CENTRE

30 ⭐ MAP P64, A5

This living-room venue expanded for noise rockers has a great *café* (pub). In the back, behind

the bookcase-concealed door, the main room has a stage and screens cult movies (in English) on Monday. DJs, vaudeville-type acts and comedy shows are also on the eclectic agenda. (www.denieuweanita.nl; Frederik Hendrikstraat 111; 🚊3 Hugo de Grootplein)

Movies CINEMA

31 ⭐ MAP P64, D1

Amsterdam's oldest cinema, dating from 1912, is a *gezellig* (cosy) gem screening indie films alongside mainstream flicks. Tickets are €1 cheaper online. You can dine in the pan-Asian restaurant (open 5.30pm to 10pm) or have a pre-film tipple at the inviting *café*. (☎020-638 60 16; www.themovies.nl; Haarlemmerdijk 161; tickets €11.50; 🚊3 Haarlemmerplein)

Maloe Melo BLUES

32 ⭐ MAP P64, B7

This is the freewheeling, fun-loving altar of Amsterdam's tiny blues scene. Music ranges from funk and soul to Texas blues and rockabilly. The cover charge is usually around €5. (☎020-420 45 92; www.maloemelo.com; Lijnbaansgracht 163; ⏰9pm-3am Sun-Thu, to 4am Fri & Sat; 🚊5/17/19 Elandsgracht)

Shopping

Frozen Fountain HOMEWARES

33 🔒 MAP P64, D8

Frozen Fountain is Amsterdam's best-known showcase of furniture

Drop: Dutch Liquorice

The Dutch love their sweets, the most famous of which is *drop,* the word for all varieties of liquorice. It may be gummy-soft or tough as leather, and shaped like coins or miniature cars, but the most important distinction is between *zoete* (sweet) and *zoute* (salty). The latter is often an alarming surprise, even for avowed fans of the black stuff. But with such a range of textures and additional flavours – mint, honey, laurel – even liquorice sceptics might be converted. **Het Oud-Hollandsch Snoepwinkeltje** (Map p64, C4; www.snoepwinkeltje.com; 2e Egelantiersdwarsstraat 2; ◷11am-6.30pm Tue-Sat; 🚊3/5 Marnixplein) is a good place to do a taste test.

and interior design. Prices are not cheap, but the daring designs are offbeat and very memorable (designer penknives, kitchen gadgets and that birthday gift for the impossible-to-wow friend). Best of all, it's an unpretentious place where you can browse at length without feeling uncomfortable. (www.frozenfountain.com; Prinsengracht 645; ◷1-6pm Mon, 10am-6pm Tue-Sat, noon-5pm Sun; 🚊2/11/12 Prinsengracht)

Moooi Gallery

DESIGN

34 🔒 MAP P64, C3

Founded by Dutch designer Marcel Wanders, this gallery-shop features Dutch design at its most over-the-top, from the life-size black horse lamp to the 'blow away vase' (a whimsical twist on the classic Delft vase) and the 'killing of the piggy bank' ceramic pig (with a gold hammer). (📞020-528 77 60; www.moooi.com; Westerstraat 187; ◷10am-6pm Tue-Sat; 🚊3/5 Marnixplein)

Memento

DESIGN

35 🔒 MAP P64, C6

Levitating lamps and vases (using magnets), retro flipping clocks, Delft-style porcelain with contemporary designs such as cyclists and tilting canal houses, gable-shaped chopping boards, wine coolers made from leather offcuts, Dutch flower-scented perfumes, tulip- and green parrot-printed boxer shorts, and Van Gogh–printed scarves are just some of the ingenious items by Amsterdam designers at this original boutique. (www.memento.amsterdam; Prinsengracht 238; ◷3-7pm Wed-Sun; 🚊13/17 Westermarkt)

360 Volt

HOMEWARES

36 🔒 MAP P64, D6

One of the keys to creating a quintessentially *gezellig* (cosy, convivial) atmosphere is ambient lighting, making this shop stocking vintage industrial lighting (restored to meet energy-efficient

international standards) a real find. Its lights grace some of the world's hottest bars, restaurants, hotels and film sets, such as the James Bond instalment *Spectre*. Worldwide shipping can be arranged. (☎020-810 01 01; www.360volt.com; Prinsengracht 397; ⏰11am-6pm Thu-Sat; 🚊13/17 Westermarkt)

Marie-Stella-Maris COSMETICS

37 🔒 MAP P64, D7

Marie-Stella-Maris was set up as a social enterprise to provide clean drinking water worldwide. It donates a percentage from every purchase of its locally bottled mineral waters and its aromatic plant-based skincare products (body lotions, hand soaps, shea butter) and home fragrances (travel pillow sprays, scented candles) to support its cause. Its basement cafe–water bar opens at weekends. (www.marie-stella-maris.com; Keizersgracht 357; ⏰10am-6pm Tue-Sat, noon-6pm Sun & Mon; 🚊2/11/12 Keizersgracht)

Vanilia FASHION & ACCESSORIES

38 🔒 MAP P64, D7

Dutch label Vanilia only designs limited editions, so you're unlikely to find the same styles here twice. Along with women's clothing (tops, trousers, dresses, skirts and jumpsuits), it also has lingerie, hats, belts, shoes, sunglasses, bags and jewellery, many made from salvaged offcuts of materials to reduce its environmental footprint. (www.vanilia.com; Runstraat 9; ⏰10am-6pm Tue, Wed, Fri & Sat,

Marie-Stella-Maris

to 7pm Thu, noon-6pm Sun & Mon; 🚊2/12 Keizersgracht)

Arnold Cornelis

FOOD

39 🔒 MAP P64, C7

Your dinner hosts will be impressed if you present them with something from this long-standing shop, such as fruitcake, cheesecake or biscuits made with Malaga wine. At lunchtime grab a flaky pastry filled with cheese, meat or vegetables. (📞020-625 85 85; www.cornelis.nl; Elandsgracht 78; ⏰8.30am-6pm Mon-Fri, to 5pm Sat; 🚊7/17 Elandsgracht)

Zipper

VINTAGE

40 🔒 MAP P64, D7

Seriously nostalgic, retro secondhand gear here might include wacky printed shirts, stovepipe jeans, '40s zoot suits and pork-pie hats. The shop is restocked twice weekly. (www.zippervintageclothing. com; Huidenstraat 7; ⏰noon-6.30pm Mon, 11am-6.30pm Tue, Wed, Fri & Sat, 11am-8pm Thu, 1-6.30pm Sun; 🚊2/11/12 Spui)

Urban Cacao

CHOCOLATE

41 🔒 MAP P64, B6

Chocolatier, patissier and glacier Hans Mekking is the mastermind behind Urban Cacao. Filled with his chocolate bars, truffles and pralines using fair-trade beans (with sugar-free varieties), the stylish space also has colourful macarons (such as passion fruit and chocolate, mandarin and basil, and orange and gold dust for King's Day), plus ice cream in summer and hot chocolate in winter. (www.

Fish stall at Lindengracht Market

PROTASOV AN/SHUTTERSTOCK ©

Neighbourhood Markets

The **Lindengracht Market** (Map p64, D2; www.jordaanmarkten.nl; Lindengracht; ⏰9am-4pm Sat; 🚊3 Nieuwe Willemsstraat) is a wonderfully authentic local affair, with bountiful fresh produce, including fish and magnificent cheese stalls, as well as gourmet goods, clothing and homewares. Arrive as early as possible for the best pickings and smallest crowds.

Another good one for treasure hunters is the **Westermarkt** (Map p64, D3; www.jordaanmarkten.nl; Westerstraat; ⏰9am-1pm Mon; 🚊3/5 Marnixplein), where bargain-priced clothing and fabrics are sold at 170 stalls; note it isn't in fact on Westermarkt but on Westerstraat, just near the **Noordermarkt** (p63).

facebook.com/UrbanCacao; Rozengracht 200; ⏰10am-6.30pm Tue-Sat, noon-6.30pm Sun & Mon; 🚊5/13/17/19 Marnixstraat/Rozengracht)

Robins Hood   DESIGN

42 🔒 MAP P64, C4

Whitewashed walls and floorboards create a blank canvas for the upcycled vintage and Dutch-designed products here. Browse for unique items including vases, bags, scarves, jewellery, sunglasses, lamps, art, stationery and some truly only-in-the-Netherlands items such as *stroopwafel* coasters. (www.robinshood.nl; 2e Tuindwarsstraat 7; ⏰noon-5pm Mon-Sat; 🚊3/5 Marnixplein)

Papabubble   FOOD

43 🔒 MAP P64, D1

This hip sweetshop looks more like a gallery. Pull up a cushion

and perch on the stairs to watch the mesmerising process of transforming sugar into sweets with flavours such as pomelo and lavender. (📞020-626 26 62; www.papabubble.nl; Haarlemmerdijk 70; ⏰noon-6pm Wed, 10am-6pm Sat; 🚊3 Haarlemmerplein)

Mechanisch Speelgoed   TOYS

44 🔒 MAP P64, D3

This adorable shop is crammed full of nostalgic toys, including snow domes, glow lamps, masks, finger puppets and wind-up toys. And who doesn't need a good rubber chicken every once in a while? Hours can vary. (www.mechanisch-speelgoed.nl; Westerstraat 67; ⏰10am-6pm Mon-Fri, to 5pm Sat; 🚊3/5 Marnixplein)

Walking Tour 🚶

**Westerpark &
Western Islands**

*A reedy wilderness, a post-industrial culture
complex and a drawbridge-filled adventure await
those who make the trip here. Architectural and
foodie hotspots add to the hip, eco-urban mash-
up. The area's rags-to-riches story is prototypical
Amsterdam: abandoned factoryland hits the
skids, squatters salvage it, and it rises again in
creative fashion.*

Getting There

This area borders the
Jordaan to the northwest;
it's a 3.8km walk in all.

🚊 Tram 3 and 10 swing by
the area.

🚌 22 goes to Het Schip.

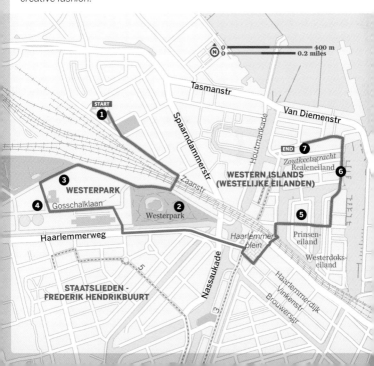

❶ Architecture

Remarkable housing project **Het Schip** (☎020-686 85 95; www.hetschip.nl; Oostzaanstraat 45; tour adult/child €15/5; ⏱11am-5pm Tue-Sun, English tour 3pm; ☐22 Spaarndammerstraat) is the pinnacle of Amsterdam School architecture. Michel de Klerk designed the triangular block, loosely resembling a ship, for railway employees. There is a small museum.

❷ Patch of Green

The pond-dappled green space **Westerpark** (Spaarndammerstraat; ☐3 Haarlemmerplein) is a cool-cat hang-out that blends into Westergasfabriek, a former gasworks transformed into an edgy cultural park, with *cafés* (pubs), theatres, breweries and other creative spaces.

❸ Terrace Drinks

On sunny afternoons young artsy professionals flock to the massive decked outdoor terrace at **Westergasterras** (www.westergasterras.nl; Klönneplein 4-6, Westergasfabriek; ⏱11am-1am Mon-Thu, to 3am Fri, 10am-3am Sat, to 1am Sun; ☎; ☐5 Van Limburg Stirumstraat). A toasty fireplace makes the cafe equally inviting indoors. Late at night on weekends it morphs into a club.

❹ Mussels & Gin

Join locals drinking gin and devouring *mosselen* (mussels) served in varieties such as crème fraîche and gin in the sunny beer gardens and soaring interior of **Mossel En Gin** (☎020-486 58 69; www.mosselengin.nl; Gosschalklaan 12, Westergasfabriek; mains €16-22; ⏱kitchen 4-10.30pm Tue-Thu, 2-10.30pm Fri, 1-10.30pm Sat & Sun, bar to midnight Tue-Thu & Sun, to 1am Fri & Sat; ☎; ☐5 Van Hallstraat).

❺ Western Islands

The **Western Islands** were originally home to shipworks and the Dutch West India Company's warehouses in the early 1600s. The district is a world unto itself, cut through with canals and linked with small drawbridges.

❻ Scenic Zandhoek

Visit photogenic **Zandhoek** (Realeneiland; ☐48 Barentszplein), a stretch of waterfront on the eastern shore. Now a yacht harbour, back in the 17th century it was a 'sand market', where ships would purchase bags of the stuff for ballast.

❼ Foodie Love at Marius

The chef of little Western Islands' restaurant **Marius** (☎020-422 78 80; www.restaurantmarius.nl; Barentszstraat 173; 4-course menu €49; ⏱6.30-10pm Mon-Sat; ☐3 Zoutkeetsgracht) shops at local markets for the ingredients used to create his daily four-course menu.

Explore
Southern
Canal Ring

The Southern Canal Ring is a horseshoe-shaped loop of parallel canals. It's home to the nightlife hubs of Leidseplein and Rembrandtplein, where bars, clubs and restaurants cluster around large squares. Between the two, the canals are lined by some of the city's most elegant houses; the area also encompasses many fine museums, a flower market and waterside restaurants and bars.

The Short List

○ **Hermitage Amsterdam (p88)** Goggling at blockbuster exhibitions drawn from the wealth of treasures at the original St Petersburg museum.

○ **Golden Bend (p85)** Ambling along the stretch of Golden Age canal-side property.

○ **Reguliersgracht (p89)** Enjoying romantic ahhs on the so-called 'canal of seven bridges'.

○ **Museum Van Loon (p89)** Getting an insight into the lavish lifestyle of Amsterdam's top rung from the Golden Age to the 19th century in this gracious canal-side abode.

○ **Museum Willet-Holthuysen (p88)** Exploring the lavishness of patrician canal-house life in this historic former family home.

Getting There & Around

🚊 This area is well-served by trams. For the Leidseplein area, take tram 1, 2, 5, 7, 11, 12 or 19. To reach Rembrandtplein, take tram 4, which travels down Utrechtsestraat, or tram 14. Tram 24 cuts through the centre of the neighbourhood down busy Vijzelstraat.

Neighbourhood Map on p86

Golden Bend (p85) S.BORISOV/SHUTTERSTOCK ©

Walking Tour 🥾

Strolling the Southern Canal Ring

Puttin' on the Ritz is nothing new to the Southern Canal Ring. Most of the area was built at the end of the 17th century when Amsterdam was wallowing in Golden Age cash. A wander through reveals grand mansions, swanky antique shops, an indulgent patisserie and a one-of-a-kind kitty museum. And while it's all stately, it's certainly not snobby.

Walk Facts
Start Flower Market
End Café Americain
Length 2km; one hour

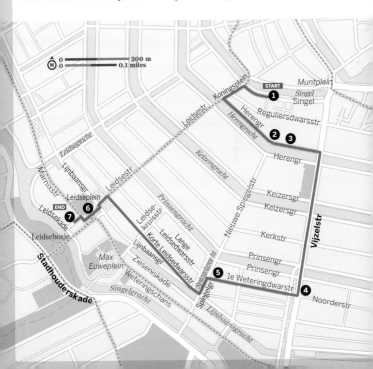

❶ Flower Market

The canal-side **Bloemenmarkt** (Flower Market; Singel, btwn Muntplein & Koningsplein; ⊙9am-5pm; 🚊2/11/12 Koningsplein) has been here since 1860. Exotic bulbs are the main stock, though cut flowers brighten the stalls, too.

❷ Golden Bend Riches

During the Golden Age, the Herengracht's **Golden Bend** (Gouden Bocht; Herengracht, btwn Leidsestraat & Vijzelstraat; 🚊2/11/12 Koningsplein) was the 'it' spot, where the wealthiest Amsterdammers lived. Many mansions here date from the 1660s; the gables were allowed to be twice as wide as the standard Amsterdam model.

❸ Odd art at the Kattenkabinet

The only Golden Bend abode that's open to the public is the **Kattenkabinet** (Cat Cabinet; 📞020-626 90 40; www.kattenkabinet.nl; Herengracht 497; adult/child €7/free; ⊙10am-5pm Mon-Fri, noon-5pm Sat & Sun; 🚻; 🚊24 Muntplein), an offbeat museum devoted to cat-related art. A Picasso drawing, kitschy kitty lithographs and odd pieces of ephemera cram the creaky old house. Happy live felines lounge on the window seats.

❹ Treats at Patisserie Holtkamp

At **Patisserie Holtkamp** (www.patisserieholtkamp.nl; Vijzelgracht 15; baked goods €3-7; ⊙8.30am-6pm Mon-Fri, to 5pm Sat; Ⓜ️Vijzelgracht, 🚊1/7/19/24 Vijzelgracht), look up to spot the gilded royal coat of arm. This swanky bakery supplies the Dutch royals with delicacies including *kroketten* (croquets) with fillings of prawns, lobster and veal.

❺ Spiegel Quarter Antiques

The perfect Delft vase or 16th-century wall map will most assuredly be hiding among the antique stores, bric-a-brac shops and commercial art galleries along Spiegelgracht and Nieuwe Spiegelstraat, aka the **Spiegel Quarter**.

❻ Theatre Time

The neo-Renaissance **Internationaal Theater Amsterdam** (📞020-624 23 11; www.ita.nl/en/; Leidseplein 26; ⊙box office noon-6pm Mon-Sat & 2hr before performances; 🚊1/2/5/7/11/12/19 Leidseplein) takes pride of place on the Leidseplein. The regal venue, built in 1894, is used for large-scale plays, operettas and more.

❼ Drinks at Café Americain

Opened in 1902, art nouveau **Café Americain** (📞020-556 30 10; www.cafeamericain.nl; Amsterdam American Hotel, Leidsekade 97; ⊙6.30am-midnight; 📶; 🚊1/2/5/7/11/12/19 Leidseplein) has huge stained-glass windows overlooking Leidseplein, a lovely, library-like reading table and a great terrace.

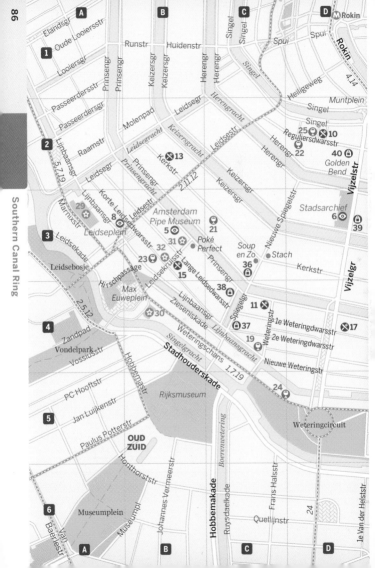

A

B

C

D Ⓜ Rokin

Elandsgr

Oude Looiersstr

Runstr

Huidenstr

Spui

Spui

Rokin

1

Looiersgr

Prinsengr

Prinsengr

Keizersgr

Keizersgr

Herengr

Herengr

Singel

4.14

Passeerdersstr

Molenpad

Leidsegr

Herengracht

Heiligeweg

Muntplein

Passeerdersgr

Raamstr

Leidsegracht

Keizersgracht

Singel

Singel

Singel

25 ⓘ ⊗ 10

Reguliersdwarsstr

2

Linbaansgr

5.7.19

Leidsegr

Prinsengracht

Kerkstr

⊗ 13

2.11.12

Keizersgr

Herengr

Herengr

22

40 ⓐ

Golden

Bend

Vijzelstr

Korte Leidsedwarsstr

Marnixstr

Lijnbaansgr

29

8 ⓐ

Leidseplein

Amsterdam

Pipe Museum

5 ⓘ

21 ⓘ

Keizersgr

Nieuwe Spiegelstr

Stadsarchief

6 ⓘ

39 ⓐ

Vijzelgr

3

Leidsekade

Leidsebosje

31 ★

32 ★

23 ⓘ

Poké

Perfect

Lange Leidsedwarsstr

15

Prinsengr

Soup

en Zo

36 ⓐ

● Stach

Kerkstr

Hirschpassage

Max

Euweplein

★ 30

Lijnbaansgr

Zieseniskade

Leidsekruisstr

38 ⓐ

Spiegelgr

11 ⊗

ⓐ 37

19

Weteringstr

1e Weteringdwarsstr

2e Weteringdwarsstr

⊗ 17

4

Zandpad

Vondelpark

Vossiusstr

Hobbemastr

Weteringschans

Singelgracht

Stadhouderskade

1.7.19

Nieuwe Weteringstr

24 ⓘ

PC Hooftstr

Jan Luijkenstr

Rijksmuseum

Weteringcircuit

5

Paulus Potterstr

OUD

ZUID

Honthorststr

Hobbemakade

Boerenwetering

Ruysdaelkade

Frans Halsstr

24

1e Van der Helststr

6

Van Baerlestr

Museumplein

Museumpl

Johannes Vermeerstr

Quellijnstr

A

B

C

D

E · F · G · H

Kloveniersburgwal
Kloveniersburgwal
Groenburgwal
Zwanenburgwal
Zwanenburgwal
Jodenbreestr
Waterlooplein
Valkenburgerstr
Mr Visserplein
Rapenburgerstr
Nieuwe Doelenstr
1
14
Muiderstr

Binnen Amstel
Stopera
35 Halvemaan-
steeg
Amstel
Waterlooplein
Weesperstr
Reguliersbreestr
27
Bakkerstr
Amstelstr
Blauwbrug
Hermitage
Amsterdam
2

28 **9**
20 Reguliersdwarsstr
Thorbeckeplein
Rembrandtplein
12 **7**
Tassenmuseum
Hendrikje
2 Museum Willet-
Holthuysen
14
1
Nieuwe Keizersgr
Nieuwe Keizersgracht
Herengr
Reguliersgracht
Herengr
Utrechtsestr

4
Foam
16
Keizersgr
Keizersgr
Keizersgracht
Nieuwe Kerkstr
Magere
Brug
Amstel
Nieuwe
Prinsengracht
3

3
Keizersgr
Museum
Van Loon
34
Kerkstr
Lepelstr
Reguliersgr
Prinsengr
33
Nieuwe Achtergr
Amstel

26 Amstelveld
Prinsengracht
Prinsengr
Prinsengr
Utrechtsedwarsstr
41
Achtergr
Amstel
18
4

Noorderstr
Nieuwe Looiersstr
Fokke Simonszstr
Utrechtsedwarsstr
Falckstr
Frederiksplein
Sarphatistr
Sarphatistr

Weteringschans
Reguliersgracht
Nicolaas Witsenstr
1,7,19
Westeinde
5

Den Texstr
Nieuwe Witsenkade
Sarphatikade
Singelgracht
N 0 ——— 200 m
0 ——— 0.1 miles

Stadhouderskade

2e Jacob van
Campenstr
Hemonylaan
Van Woustr
Govert Flinckstr

For reviews see	
◉ Sights	p88
✖ Eating	p91
Drinking	p94
☆ Entertainment	p96
🔒 Shopping	p98

6

Quellijnstr
Gerard Doustr
Albert Cuypstr
2e Jan Steenstr

E · F · G · H

Sights

Hermitage Amsterdam

MUSEUM

1 ⊙ MAP P86, G2

There have long been links between Russia and the Netherlands – Tsar Peter the Great learned shipbuilding here in 1697 – hence this branch of St Petersburg's State Hermitage Museum. Blockbuster temporary exhibitions show works from the Hermitage's vast treasure trove, while the permanent Portrait Gallery of the Golden Age has formal group portraits of the 17th-century Dutch A-list; the Outsider Gallery also has temporary shows. I Amsterdam and Museum cards allow free entrance or a discount, depending on the exhibition. (☎020-530 87 55; www.hermitage.nl; Amstel 51; single exhibitions adult/child €18/free; all exhibitions adult/child €25/free; ⊙10am-5pm; ♿; Ⓜ Waterlooplein, 🚊14 Waterlooplein)

Museum Willet-Holthuysen

MUSEUM

2 ⊙ MAP P86, F2

This exquisite canal house was built in 1687 for Amsterdam mayor Jacob Hop, then remodelled in 1739. It's named after Louisa Willet-Holthuysen, who inherited the house from her coal-and-glass-merchant father and lived a lavish, bohemian life here with her husband. She bequeathed the property to the city in 1895. With displays including part of

Hermitage Amsterdam

MARTIN BERGSMA/SHUTTERSTOCK ©

Photographing the Seven Bridges

It's easy to get swept away in the raucous local nightlife and forget that one of Amsterdam's most romantic canals flows through this neighbourhood. The **Reguliersgracht** (Map p86, E3; 🚋4/14 Rembrandtplein), aka the 'canal of seven bridges', is especially enchanting by night, when its humpbacked arches glow with tiny gold lights.

Though the best views are from aboard a boat, you can still get great vistas from land. Stand with your back to the Thorbeckeplein and with the Herengracht flowing directly in front of you to the left and right. Lean over the bridge and look straight ahead down the Reguliersgracht. Ahhh. Now kiss your sweetie.

the family's 275-piece Meissen table service, and an immaculate French-style garden, the museum is a fascinating window into the 19th-century world of the super-rich. (📞020-523 18 70; www.willetholthuysen.nl; Herengracht 605; adult/child €12.50/free; ⏰10am-5pm; 🚋4/14 Rembrandtplein)

Museum Van Loon   MUSEUM

3 ⊙ MAP P86, E3

An insight into life at the top of the pile in the 19th century, Museum Van Loon is an opulent 1672 residence that was first home to painter Ferdinand Bol and later to the wealthy Van Loon family. Important paintings such as *The Marriage of Willem van Loon and Margaretha Bas* by Jan Miense Molenaer and a collection of some 150 portraits of the Van Loons hang inside sumptuous interiors. (📞020-624 52 55; www.museumvanloon.nl; Keizersgracht 672; adult/child €10/5.50, free

with Museum & I Amsterdam cards; ⏰10am-5pm; 🚋4 Keizersgracht)

Foam   GALLERY

4 ⊙ MAP P86, E3

From the outside, it looks like a grand canal house, but this is the city's most important photography gallery. Its simple, spacious galleries, some with skylights or large windows for natural light, host four major exhibitions annually, featuring world-renowned photographers such as William Eggleston and Helmut Newton. There's a **cafe** in the basement. (Fotografiemuseum Amsterdam; www.foam.org; Keizersgracht 609; adult/child €12.50/free; ⏰10am-6pm Sat-Wed, to 9pm Thu & Fri; 🚋4 Keizersgracht)

Amsterdam Pipe Museum   MUSEUM

5 ⊙ MAP P86, B3

This museum is located in the grand 17th-century canal house

Crowd Control

Amsterdam's visitor numbers are skyrocketing, with 19 million tourists in 2018 alone – an astonishing figure given the city's 867,000-strong population.

Quantity isn't the only concern; quality is an issue too, with throngs of hard-partying visitors disturbing residential neighbourhoods, short-term apartment rentals driving rents and property prices up, and local shops and community services being displaced by lucrative souvenir and snack vendors.

The city has taken the drastic step of no longer actively promoting Amsterdam as a tourist destination. But it still welcomes visitors and is introducing measures to manage the crowds.

Digital fences at nightlife hotspots like Leidseplein and Rembrandtplein will send notifications via social media to remind visitors to treat the areas and residents respectfully.

Diverting budget airlines to Lelystad Airport (50km east of Amsterdam) frees up Schiphol International Airport to handle greater passenger numbers, and also directs visitors to explore the capital's surrounds.

Socially minded initiatives like 'marrying' a local for a day and fishing plastic from the city's waterways while cruising them in boats made from the recycled waste also aim to integrate locals with visitors, and encourage travel as a force for good.

---

of the marvellously single-minded pipe collector who gathered this unexpectedly fascinating collection from around 60 different countries over 40 years. Knowledgeable guides take you through the exhibits, from the earliest South American pipes, dating from 500 BC, to 15th-century Dutch pipes, Chinese opium pipes, African ceremonial pipes and much more. A peek into the house is worth the price of admission alone. (☏ 020-421 17 79; www.pipemuseum.nl; Prinsengracht 488; adult/child €10/5; ⏱ noon-6pm Wed-Sat; 🚋 2/11/12 Prinsengracht)

Stadsarchief   MUSEUM

6 ◉ MAP P86, D3

A distinctive striped building dating from 1923, this former bank now houses 23km of shelving storing Amsterdam archives. Fascinating displays of archive gems, such as the 1942 police report on the theft of Anne Frank's bike and a letter from Charles Darwin to Artis Royal Zoo in 1868, can be viewed in the enormous tiled basement

vault. Tours (adult/child €7.50/free, 1¼ hours) run at 2pm on Sundays, and must be booked in advance. (Municipal Archives; 📱tour reservations 020-251 15 11; www.amsterdam.nl/stadsarchief; Vijzelstraat 32; admission free; 🕐10am-5pm Tue-Fri, noon-5pm Sat & Sun; 🚊24 Muntplein)

Tassenmuseum Hendrikje

MUSEUM

7 ◉ MAP P86, E2

This grand 17th-century canal-house museum has a covetable collection of arm candy. More than 5000 bags can be found here, including a medieval pouch, Perspex 1960s containers, design classics by Chanel, Gucci and Versace, an '80s touchtone phone bag and Madonna's ivy-strewn 'Evita' bag from the film's premiere. The **cafe** has pricey-but-nice high teas and cakes. (Museum of Bags & Purses; 📱020-524 64 52; www.tassenmuseum.nl; Herengracht 573; adult/child €13/4; 🕐10am-5pm; 🚊4/14 Rembrandtplein)

Leidseplein

SQUARE

8 ◉ MAP P86, A3

Historic architecture, beer, clubs and steakhouses – welcome to Leidseplein. The square is always busy, but after dark it gets thronged by a mainstream crowd of party lovers (more tourists than locals). A major hub for nightlife and trams, it has countless pubs and clubs, masses of restaurants and an aroma of roasted meat. Pavement cafes at the northern

end are perfect for people-watching. Entertainment venues line the streets around the square; nearby Kerkstraat has a cluster of gay venues. (🚊1/2/5/7/11/12/19 Leidseplein)

Eating

Van Dobben

DUTCH €

9 🍴 MAP P86, E2

Open since the 1940s, Van Dobben has a cool diner feel, with white tiles and a siren-red ceiling. Traditional meaty Dutch fare is its forte: low-priced, finely sliced roast-beef sandwiches with mustard are an old-fashioned joy, or try the *pekelvlees* (akin to corned beef) or *halfom* (if you're keen on *pekelvlees* mixed with liver). (📱020-624 42 00; www.eetsalonvandobben.nl; Korte Reguliersdwarsstraat 5-9; dishes €3-8; 🕐10am-9pm Mon-Thu, to 2am Fri & Sat, 10.30am-8pm Sun; 📶; 🚊4/14 Rembrandtplein)

Vegan Junk Food Bar

VEGAN €€

10 🍴 MAP P86, D2

This flashy restaurant, vaunting pink graffiti walls and neon lights, serves healthy 'junk' food. Plant-based burgers are the best-known fare, but you can also order sashimi made from tapioca, fruity cocktails and CBD-infused juice. (www.veganjunkfoodbar.com; Reguliersdwarsstraat 57; mains €9-15; 🕐11am-1am Sun-Thu, to 3am Fri & Sat; 📶📱; 🚊24 Muntplein)

Buffet van Odette

CAFE €€

11 🍴 MAP P86, C4

Chow down at Odette's, a white-tiled cafe with an enchanting canal-side location, where delicious dishes are made with great ingredients and a dash of creativity. Try the splendid platter of cured meats, or mains such as ravioli with pumpkin, sage and hazelnut, or smoked salmon, lentils and poached egg. (📞020-423 60 34; www.buffet-amsterdam.nl; Prinsengracht 598; mains €9-18.50; 🕐noon-midnight Wed-Mon; 🍴; 🚊1/7/19 Spiegelgracht)

Guts

EUROPEAN €€€

12 🍴 MAP P86, F2

Guts' four-course menu is constantly changing and customisable with add-on à la carte options, like razor clams and charcuterie. The focus is on sustainable, regional products with little flourishes, and for lunch you can even share a whole turbot. Exposed bulbs and white-brick walls keep things sophisticated. (📞020-362 00 30; www.bredagroup-amsterdam.com/guts; Utrechtsestraat 6; menu €42.50, extra dishes €5-18; 🕐noon-3pm & 6-10pm; 🚊4/14 Rembrandtplein)

Ron Gastrobar Oriental

ASIAN €€

13 🍴 MAP P86, B2

Michelin-starred chef Ron Blaauw began his food revolution at Ron Gastrobar (p114) near Vondelpark, introducing a one-price menu of tapas-style dishes so diners could eat fine cuisine without settling down for a long formal meal. This is his Asian version. The menu includes delicacies such as dim sum of steamed scallop with Chinese mushroom and crispy prawns with wasabi mayo. (📞020-223 53 52; www.rongastrobar oriental.nl; Kerkstraat 23; dim sum €8.50, mains €17.50; 🕐5.30-11pm; 📶; 🚊2/11/12 Prinsengracht)

Dignita Hoftuin

CAFE €€

14 🍴 MAP P86, H2

Set in the garden behind the Hermitage (p88), this cafe serves a brunchy menu of Ottolenghi-style salads, sandwiches and light snacks. Its walls are glass, and the place is flooded with light; there are also chairs and tables outside. It's a dreamy spot on a sunny summer's day. (www.eatwelldogood. nl; Nieuwe Herengracht 18a; dishes €8-14; 🕐9am-6pm; 🍴🚼; 🚇Waterlooplein; 🚊14 Waterlooplein)

Pantry

DUTCH €€

15 🍴 MAP P86, B3

With wood-panelled walls and sepia lighting, this little restaurant is *gezellig* (cosy, convivial) indeed. Tuck into classic Dutch dishes such as *zuurkool stamppot* (sauerkraut and potato mash served with a smoked sausage or meatball) or *hutspot* ('hotch-potch', with stewed beef, carrots and onions). (📞020-620 09 22; www.thepantry.nl; Leidsekruisstraat

CLAIRE BISSELL/LONELY PLANET ©

Traditional Dutch food at Van Dobben (p91)

21; mains €13.75-20, 3-course menus €21.50-31.25; ⏱11am-10.30pm; 🚋1/2/5/7/11/12/19 Leidseplein)

Café van Leeuwen

BRASSERIE €€

16 MAP P86, F3

Bruin café (traditional Dutch pub) in style, with lots of dark-wooded charm, dangling light bulbs and an exposed brick wall, this spot offers fine brasserie-style dishes such as succulent hamburgers and open sandwiches. It's a great place for breakfast or brunch, and the canal-side setting is fabulous. (www.cafevanleeuwen.nl; Keizersgracht 711; mains €7-17; ⏱8am-10pm Mon-Sat, to 9pm Sun; 🚋4 Keizersgracht)

Piet de Leeuw

STEAK €€

17 MAP P86, D4

With its dark-wood furniture and wood-panelled walls hung with pictures, this feels like an old-school pub. The building dates from 1900, but it's been a steakhouse and a hang-out since the 1940s. Sit down at individual or communal tables and tuck into good-value steaks topped with a choice of sauces and served with salad and piping-hot *frites* (French fries). (📞020-623 71 81; www.pietdeleeuw.nl; Noorderstraat 11; mains €13-25; ⏱noon-10.30pm Mon-Fri, 5-10.30pm Sat & Sun; 🚋4 Prinsengracht)

Healthy Fast Food

The Southern Canal Ring has plenty of fast-food outlets. For a healthy bite on the run, try **Poké Perfect** (Map p86, B3; www.pokeperfect. com; Prinsengracht 502; mains around €10; ⏰11.30am-9pm; 🚊; 🚋1/2/5/7/11/12/19 Leidseplein) for poké bowls, **Soup en Zo** (Map p86, C3; www.soupenzo. nl; Nieuwe Spiegelstraat 54; soup €4.50-8; ⏰11am-8pm Mon-Fri, noon-7pm Sat & Sun; 🚊; 🚋1/7/19 Spiegelgracht) for steaming soups or deli/cafe **Stach** (Map p86, C3; www.stachfood.nl; Nieuwe Spiegelstraat 52; dishes €7.50-15; ⏰8am-10pm Mon-Sat, 9am-9pm Sun; 🚊; 🚋1/7/19 Spiegelgracht) for fantastic gourmet sandwiches.

Drinking

Bakhuys Amsterdam CAFE

18 MAP P86, H4

In this large industrial space, watch from up close as bakers knead dough and work the wood-fired oven. Benches provide ample space for coffee dates or laptop work fuelled by pastries and sweets. (📞020-370 48 61; www.bakhuys-amsterdam.nl; Sarphatistraat 61; ⏰7am-7pm Mon-Sat, 8am-5pm Sun; 🛜; Ⓜ Weesperplein, 🚊Weesperplein)

Back to Black CAFE

19 MAP P86, C4

It's easy to lose track of time in this ultra-cool neighbourhood cafe with teal walls and exposed light bulbs and wood shelves hanging on ropes. Back to Black chooses its beans with care and roasts them locally in Amsterdam. It also serves a small but stellar selection of cakes and pastries. (📞020-304 49 88; www.backtoblackcoffee.nl; Weteringstraat 48; ⏰8am-6pm Mon-Fri, from 9am Sat & Sun; 🛜; 🚋1/7/19 Spiegelgracht)

Door 74 COCKTAIL BAR

20 MAP P86, E2

You'll need to send a text or WhatsApp for a reservation to gain entry to this speakeasy behind an unmarked door. Some of Amsterdam's most amazing cocktails are served in a classy, dark-timbered Prohibition-era atmosphere beneath pressed-tin ceilings. Themed cocktail lists change regularly. Very cool. (📞020-634 04 51 22; www.door-74.nl; Reguliersdwarsstraat 74; ⏰8pm-3am Sun-Thu, to 4am Fri & Sat; 🚊4/14 Rembrandtplein)

Bocca Coffee COFFEE

21 MAP P86, C3

The team behind Bocca Coffee knows its stuff, having sourced beans from Ethiopia to sell to cafes across the city for more than 15 years. It's now serving some

seriously good caffeine hits in this light, spacious coffeehouse. Take a seat at the large wooden bar or get comfy in a vintage armchair. Cash only. (www.bocca.nl; Kerkstraat 96; ⏰8am-6pm Mon-Fri, from 9am Sat & Sun; 🛜; 🚋2/11/12 Prinsengracht)

Lion Noir
COCKTAIL BAR

22 🚇 MAP P86, D2

Lion Noir hosts a glamorous crowd, here for excellent cocktails as well as superlative dining on creative French-inspired dishes with an Asian twist. Interior artist Thijs Murré designed the eclectic, satisfyingly out-there interior of green walls, plants, birdcages and taxidermied birds; the greenery-shaded terrace is equally lovely. (📞020-627 66 03; www.lionnoir.nl; Reguliersdwarsstraat 28; ⏰6pm-1am Sun-Thu, to 3am Fri & Sat; 🚋2/11/12 Koningsplein)

Club Up
CLUB

23 🚇 MAP P86, B3

Garage, house, funk, soul, hip-hop, techno, live bands and performance art keep the punters happy at this small, quirky club. Entrance is occasionally through social club De Kring, at Kleine Gartmanplantsoen 7–9; check the Club Up website for details. (📞020-623 69 85; www.clubup.nl; Korte Leidsedwarsstraat 26; ⏰11pm-4am Thu, to 5am Fri & Sat; 🚋1/2/5/7/11/12/19 Leidseplein)

Café Brecht
BAR

24 🚇 MAP P86, C5

Café Brecht is one of Amsterdam's loveliest bars, with mismatched armchairs, vintage furniture, books and board games; all are a hit with a young and gorgeously boho crowd – it gets absolutely crammed in here. It's named after seminal German dramatist and poet Bertolt Brecht, hence the German poetry inscribed on the walls. (📞020-627 22 11; www.cafebrecht.nl; Weteringschans 157; ⏰11am-1am Sun-Thu, to 3am Fri & Sat; Ⓜ Vijzelgracht, 🚋1/7/19/24 Vijzelgracht)

Taboo Bar
GAY

25 🚇 MAP P86, D2

Gay favourite Taboo has plentiful two-for-one happy hours (6pm to 8pm and 1am to 2am). It's snug inside, though on warmer days everyone spills out onto the street. On Wednesdays, cocktails cost €6 and a drag show and competitions like 'pin the tail on the sailor' take place. (www.taboobar.nl; Reguliersdwarsstraat 45; ⏰5pm-3am Mon-Thu, to 4am Fri, 4pm-4am Sat, to 3am Sun; 🛜; 🚋2/11/12 Koningsplein)

Brasserie NeL
BAR

26 🚇 MAP P86, F4

NeL, a stately white house on a hidden-away square, is a contender for having the best terrace in Amsterdam. Outside, mature trees provide a canopy that dapples the sunshine on a good day. Inside, there's a mellow

Utrechtsestraat: A Local Hangout

A stone's throw south from gaudy Rembrandtplein, **Utrechtsestraat** is a relaxed artery stocked with enticing shops, designer bars and cosy eateries – a prime place to wander and discover a great local hangout. The street's southern end used to terminate at the Utrechtse Poort, a gate to the nearby city of Utrecht, hence the name.

brasserie on one side and a stylish bar on the other. (📞 020-626 11 99; www.brasserienel.nl; Amstelveld 12; ⏰ 10am-1am Sun-Thu, to 3am Fri & Sat; 🛜; 🚊 4 Prinsengracht)

Montmartre
GAY

27 🟢 MAP P86, E2

A crammed gay bar that's long been a local favourite. It's known for its Dutch music, and patrons sing (or scream) along to recordings of Dutch ballads and old top-40 hits. There's also a lively programme of karaoke, drag, and '80s and '90s hits. (www.cafemontmartre.nl; Halvemaansteeg 17; ⏰ 5pm-3am Sun-Thu, to 4am Fri & Sat; 🚊 4/14 Rembrandtplein)

Entertainment

Pathé Tuschinskitheater
CINEMA

28 ⭐ MAP P86, E2

This fantastical cinema, with a facade that's a prime example of

the Amsterdam School of architecture, is worth visiting for its sumptuous art deco interior alone. The *grote zaal* (main auditorium) is the most stunning; it generally screens blockbusters, while the smaller theatres play art-house and indie films. Visit the interior on an audio tour (€10) when films aren't playing. (www.pathe.nl; Reguliersbreestraat 26-34; €11; ⏰ 9.30am-12.30am; 🚊 4/14 Rembrandtplein)

Melkweg
LIVE MUSIC

29 ⭐ MAP P86, A3

In a former dairy, the nonprofit 'Milky Way' offers a dazzling galaxy of diverse gigs, featuring both DJs and live bands. One night it's electronica, the next reggae or punk, and the next heavy metal. Roots, rock and mellow singer-songwriters all get stage time too. Check out the website for information on its cutting-edge cinema, theatre and multimedia offerings. (Milky Way; 📞 020-531 81 81; www.melkweg.nl; Lijnbaansgracht 234a; admission varies; 🚊 1/2/5/7/11/12/19 Leidseplein)

Paradiso
LIVE MUSIC

30 ⭐ MAP P86, B4

In 1968 a beautiful old church turned into the 'Cosmic Relaxation Center Paradiso'. Today, the vibe is less hippy than funked-up odyssey, with big all-nighters, themed events and indie nights. The smaller hall hosts up-and-coming bands, but there's something special about the Main Hall,

where it seems the stained-glass windows might shatter under the force of the fat beats. (📞020-622 45 21; www.paradiso.nl; Weteringschans 6-8; admission varies; 📶; 🚋1/2/5/7/11/12/19 Leidseplein)

Bourbon Street Jazz & Blues Club

LIVE MUSIC

31 ⭐ MAP P86, B3

This intimate venue has a full and eclectic weekly music programme. Take part in open jam sessions on Mondays, or come by on Tuesdays for soul and reggae. It offers blues and rock on Wednesdays; funk on Thursdays; rock, pop and Latin on Fridays; pre-rock on Saturdays; and world, folk and samba on Sundays. (www.bourbonstreet.nl; Leidsekruisstraat 6-8; admission

varies; 🕐11pm-4am Sun-Thu, to 5am Fri & Sat; 🚋2/11/12 Prinsengracht)

Jazz Café Alto

JAZZ

32 ⭐ MAP P86, B3

This is an intimate, atmospheric *bruin café*–style venue for serious jazz and (occasionally) blues. There are live gigs nightly. Doors open at 9pm, but music starts around 10pm – get here early if you want to snag a seat. (www.jazz-cafe-alto.nl; Korte Leidsedwarsstraat 115; 🕐9pm-3am Sun-Thu, to 4am Fri & Sat; 🚋1/2/5/7/11/12/19 Leidseplein)

Koninklijk Theater Carré

PERFORMING ARTS

33 ⭐ MAP P86, H4

The Carré family started their career with a horse act at the

Musician from band Danko Jones performing at Melkweg

annual fair, progressing to this circus theatre in 1887. The classical facade is richly decorated with faces of jesters, dancers and theatre folk. It hosts a great programme of quality music and theatre; the Christmas circus is a seasonal highlight. (☎0900 25 25 255; www.carre.nl; Amstel 115-125; admission varies; � box office 4-6pm; Ⓜ Weesperplein, 🚊1/7/19 Weesperplein)

Shopping

Concerto   MUSIC

34 🔒 MAP P86, F3

This rambling shop is muso heaven, with a fabulous selection of new and secondhand vinyl and CDs encompassing every imaginable genre, including rockabilly, classical and more. It's good value and has listening facilities, plus a sofa-strewn, living-room-style cafe and regular live sessions – see the website for details. (☎020-261 26 10; www.concerto.amsterdam/en; Utrechtsestraat 52-60; ☺10am-6pm Mon, Wed, Fri & Sat, to 7pm Thu, noon-6pm Sun; 🚊4 Keizersgracht)

Vlieger   STATIONERY

35 🔒 MAP P86, E2

Love stationery and paper? Make a beeline for Vlieger. Since 1869, this two-storey shop has been supplying it all: Egyptian papyrus, beautiful handmade papers from Asia and Central America, papers inlaid with flower petals or bamboo, and paper textured like snakeskin.

(☎020-623 58 34; www.vliegerpapier. nl; Amstel 34; ☺noon-6pm Mon, 9am-6pm Tue-Fri, 11am-5.30pm Sat; 🚊4/14 Rembrandtplein)

Kramer Kunst & Antiek   ANTIQUES

36 🔒 MAP P86, C3

Specialising in antique blue-and-white Dutch tiles, this engrossing, crammed-to-the-rafters shop is chock-a-block with fascinating antiques, silver candlesticks, crystal decanters, jewellery and pocket watches. It's now run by the third-generation of Kramers, brothers Sebastian and Eduard. (☎020-626 11 16; www.antique-tileshop.nl; Prinsengracht 807; ☺10am-6pm Mon-Fri, to 7pm Sat, 1-6pm Sun; 🚊1/7/19 Spiegelgracht)

Hoogkamp Antiquariaat   ANTIQUES

37 🔒 MAP P86, C4

On quaint Spiegelgracht, this antiques shop sells prints that make for great souvenirs. You'll find old maps and landscapes of Amsterdam, artworks, and quirky surprises like nature photography and scientific diagrams – just shuffle through the display stacks. (☎020-625 88 52; www.prenten.net; Spiegelgracht 27; ☺1-6pm; 🚊1/7/19 Spiegelgracht)

Tinkerbell   TOYS

38 🔒 MAP P86, C4

The mechanical bear blowing bubbles outside this shop fascinates

kids, as do the intriguing technical and scientific toys inside. You'll also find historical costumes, plush toys and a section for babies. (020-625 88 30; www.tinkerbelltoys.nl; Spiegelgracht 10; 1-6pm Mon, 10am-6pm Tue-Sat, noon-5pm Sun; 1/7/19 Spiegelgracht)

Skateboards Amsterdam
SPORTS & OUTDOORS

39 MAP P86, D3

Skater-dude heaven, with everything required for the freewheeling lifestyle: cruisers, longboards, shoes, laces, caps, beanies, bags, backpacks, and clothing including Spitfire and Thrasher T-shirts and a fantastic selection of band T-shirts. (020-421 20 96; www.skateboardsamsterdam.nl; Vijzelstraat 77; 1-6pm Sun & Mon, 11am-6pm Tue-Sat; 24 Muntplein)

Shirt Shop
CLOTHING

40 MAP P86, D2

On Amsterdam's main gay street, this shop has a kaleidoscopic array of the go-to going-out garb for many local men: nicely patterned smart shirts, as well as some funky T-shirts featuring Mexican skulls and more. (020-423 20 88; www.shirtshopamsterdam.com; Reguliers-dwarsstraat 64; 1-7pm; 24 Muntplein)

Symbol of Amsterdam

The city's symbol, XXX, appears on its coat of arms, flag (two horizontal red stripes with a central black stripe with three diagonal white St Andrew's crosses), municipal buildings and merchandising everywhere. It originated in 1505 when Amsterdam was a fishing town (St Andrew is the patron saint of fisherman).

MaisonNL
HOMEWARES

41 MAP P86, F4

This little concept store sells all sorts of beautiful things you didn't realise you needed, such as Christian Lacroix notebooks and cute-as-a-button mouse toys in matchboxes by Maileg. There's a clothing rack down the back. (www.maisonnl.com; Utrechtsestraat 118; 1-6pm Mon, 10am-6pm Tue-Sat, 1-5pm Sun; 4 Prinsengracht)

Explore ⊕
Vondelpark
& the South

The Vondelpark has a special place in Amsterdam's heart, a lush green egalitarian space where everyone hangs out at some point: local and visiting families, cyclists, picnickers and sunbathers. Nearby Museumplein is home to the Rijksmuseum, Van Gogh and Stedelijk museums. In the north you'll find cultural centre De Hallen and hip Overtoom, crammed with cafes, restaurants and bars.

The Short List

○ **Rijksmuseum (p102)** *Getting happily lost amid the riches of one of the world's finest museums.*

○ **Van Gogh Museum (p106)** *Seeing the world's best collection of Van Gogh's work up close, from vibrant yellow sunflowers to purple-blue irises.*

○ **Vondelpark (p110)** *Freewheeling through the green heart of the city.*

○ **Stedelijk Museum (p113)** *Discovering works by Mondrian, Matisse, Warhol, Appel, De Kooning, Yayoi Kusama and more at Amsterdam's fabulous modern art museum.*

○ **De Hallen (p119)** *Dining at the food hall inside this cultural centre in repurposed tram sheds.*

Getting There & Around
🚊 Trams 12 and 5 stop at Museumplein and the Vondelpark's main entrance; tram 2 travels along the park's southern side on Willemsparkweg. Trams 3 and 12 cross the 1e Constantijn Huygensstraat bridge near the park's main entrance, and Kinkerstraat near De Hallen. Tram 1 travels along Overtoom.

Neighbourhood Map on p112

Top Experience 📷
Admire Art at Rijksmuseum

The Rijksmuseum is a magnificent repository of art, its restaurant has a Michelin star and it's the only museum with a cycle lane through its centre. Beautifully presented, it includes masterpieces by homegrown geniuses, such as Rembrandt, Vermeer and Van Gogh. It was conceived to hold several national and royal collections, which occupy 1.5km of gallery space.

◎ MAP P112, E2

National Museum

☎ 020-674 70 00

www.rijksmuseum.nl

Museumstraat 1

adult/child €20/free

🕙 9am-5pm

🚊 2/5/12 Rijksmuseum

Floor 2: 1600–1700

It's best to start your visit on the 2nd floor, which contains the highlights of the collection, with its Golden Age masterpieces, in the **Gallery of Honour**. It's a bit convoluted to reach, but well signposted.

Frans Hals

Frans Hals painted with broad brushstrokes and a fluidity that was unique for the time. *The Merry Drinker* (1628–30) shows his style in action. No one knows who the gent with the beer glass is, but it's clear he's enjoying himself after a hard day's work.

Johannes (Jan) Vermeer

This floor hosts beautiful works by Vermeer, with intimate domestic scenes, glimpses into private life, rendered in almost photographic detail. Check out the dreamy *Milkmaid* (1660; also called *The Kitchen Maid*). Notice the holes in the wall? The nail with shadow? In *Woman in Blue Reading a Letter* (1663) Vermeer shows only parts of objects, such as the tables, chairs and map, leaving the viewer to figure out the rest.

Jan Steen

Jan Steen became renowned for painting chaotic households to convey moral teachings, such as *The Merry Family* (1668). None of the drunken adults notice the little boy sneaking a taste of wine. In the 18th century the expression 'a Jan Steen household' entered the local lexicon to mean a crazy state of affairs.

Rembrandt

You'll find several wonderful works by Rembrandt, including his resigned, unflinching self-portrait as the Apostle Paul. *The Jewish Bride* (1665), showing a couple's intimate caress, impressed Van Gogh, who declared he would

★ Top Tips

○ Entrance queues can be long. Friday, Saturday and Sunday are the busiest days. It's least crowded before 10am and after 3pm.

○ Buy your ticket online to save time; while you must still wait in the outdoor queue, once inside you can proceed straight into the museum (otherwise you must stand in another queue to pay). Museumkaart and I Amsterdam cardholders get the same privilege.

✕ Take a Break

Treat yourself to a gourmet lunch or dinner at **Rijks** (☏ 020-674 75 55; mains €24-32, 3-/4-course lunch menus €42/52, 6-course dinner menu €79; ⏱ 11.30am-3pm & 5-10pm Mon-Sat, 11.30-3pm Sun), the Michelin-starred museum restaurant.

If you fancy something a bit less formal, there's a **cafe** on the mezzanine in the great entrance atrium, three espresso bars inside, and one out in the garden.

Rijksmuseum

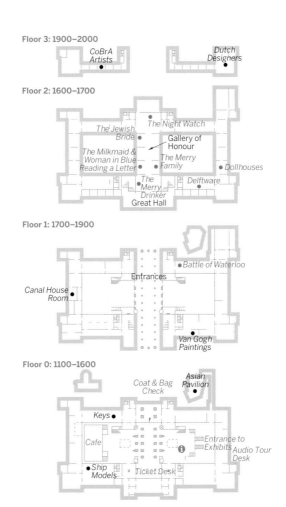

Floor 3: 1900–2000

CoBrA Artists

Dutch Designers

Floor 2: 1600–1700

The Night Watch

The Jewish Bride

Gallery of Honour

The Milkmaid & Woman in Blue Reading a Letter

The Merry Family

Dollhouses

The Merry Drinker

Delftware

Great Hall

Floor 1: 1700–1900

Battle of Waterloo

Entrances

Canal House Room

Van Gogh Paintings

Floor 0: 1100–1600

Asian Pavilion

Coat & Bag Check

Keys

Cafe

Entrance to Exhibits

Audio Tour Desk

Ship Models

Ticket Desk

give up a decade of his life just to sit before the painting for a fortnight with only a crust of bread to eat.

The Night Watch

Rembrandt's gigantic *The Night Watch* (1642) is the rock star of the Rijksmuseum, with perennial crowds in front of it. The work is titled *Archers under the Command of Captain Frans Banning Cocq,* and *The Night Watch* name was bestowed years later, thanks to a layer of grime that gave the impression it was a nocturnal scene. It's since been restored to its original colours.

Delftware

Intriguing Golden Age swag fills the rooms on either side of the Gallery of Honour. Delftware was the Dutch attempt to reproduce Chinese porcelain in the late 1600s; Gallery 2.22 displays lots of the delicate blue-and-white pottery.

Dollhouses

Gallery 2.20 is devoted to mind-blowing dollhouses. Merchant's wife Petronella Oortman employed carpenters, glassblowers and silversmiths to make the 700 items inside her dollhouse, using the same materials as they would for full-scale versions.

Floor 3: 1900–2000

The uppermost floor has a limited, but interesting, collection. It includes avant-garde, childlike paintings by Karel Appel, Constant Nieuwenhuys and their CoBrA compadres (a post-WWII movement) and cool furnishings by Dutch designers such as Gerrit Rietveld and Michel de Klerk.

Floor 1: 1700–1900

Highlights on Floor 1 include the *Battle of Waterloo,* the Rijksmuseum's largest painting (in Gallery 1.12), taking up almost an entire wall. Three Van Gogh paintings hang in Gallery 1.18. Gallery 1.16 re-creates a gilded, 18th-century canal house room.

Floor 0: 1100–1600

This floor is packed with fascinating curiosities. The **Special Collections** have sections including magic lanterns, armoury, ship models and silver miniatures. The serene **Asian Pavilion**, a separate structure that's often devoid of crowds, holds first-rate artworks from China, Indonesia, Japan, India, Thailand and Vietnam.

Facade & Gardens

Pierre Cuypers designed the 1885 building. Check out the exterior, which mixes neo-Gothic and Dutch Renaissance styles. The museum's gardens – aka the 'outdoor gallery' – host big-name sculpture exhibitions at least once a year. You can stroll for free amid the roses, hedges, fountains and a cool greenhouse.

Top Experience 📷

See the Work of a Master at the Van Gogh Museum

This wonderful museum holds the world's largest Van Gogh collection. It's a poignant experience to trace the painter's tragic yet breathtakingly productive life. Opened in 1973 to house the collection of Vincent's younger brother, Theo, the museum comprises some 200 paintings and 500 drawings by Vincent and his contemporaries, including Gauguin and Monet.

◉ MAP P112, E3

Museumplein 6
adult/child €19/free
🕙9am-7pm Sun-Thu, to 9pm Fri & Sat late Jun-Aug, 9am-6pm Sat-Thu, to 9pm Fri May–late Jun & Sep-late Oct, 9am-5pm Sat-Thu, to 9pm Fri Nov-Apr
🚋2/3/5/12 Van Baerlestraat

Museum Layout

In 2015 an extension and entrance hall added 800 sq metres of space to the museum, which now spreads over four levels, moving chronologically from Floor 0 (aka the ground floor) to Floor 3. It's still a manageable size; allow a couple of hours or so to browse the galleries.

The Potato Eaters

Van Gogh's earliest works – showing raw, if unrefined, talent – are from his time in the Dutch countryside and in Antwerp between 1883 and 1885. He painted peasant life, exalting their existence in works such as *The Potato Eaters* (1885).

Bible & Skeleton

The symbolic *Still Life with Bible* (1885), painted after his father's death, shows a burnt-out candle, his Protestant-minister father's bible and a much-thumbed smaller book, *La Joi de Vivre,* representing Van Gogh's more secular philosophy. *Skeleton with Burning Cigarette* (1886) – the print all the stoners are buying in the gift shop – was painted when Van Gogh was a student at Antwerp's Royal Academy of Fine Arts.

Self-Portraits

In 1886 Van Gogh moved to Paris, where his brother Theo was working as an art dealer. Vincent began to paint multiple self-portraits as a way of improving his portraiture without paying for models, which he was too poor to afford. He met some of the Impressionists, and his palette began to brighten.

Sunflowers

In 1888 Van Gogh left for Arles in Provence to paint its colourful landscapes. *Sunflowers* (1889) and other blossoms that shimmer with

★ Top Tips

o Prepurchase tickets online at www.van goghmuseum/nl and choose a time slot to avoid missing out, as tickets sell out days in advance.

o Museumkaart holders get free entry but still need to reserve a time slot. I Amsterdam cardholders need to reserve a time slot via the I Amsterdam website (www. iamsterdam.com); book well in advance.

o Arrive before 11am or after 3pm, or visit late on Friday to avoid the crowds.

o Audioguides cost €5 for adults and €3 for children.

✕ Take a Break

There's a **restaurant and cafe** in the Van Gogh Museum, which are nothing special but they're fine if you need a breather.

The informal, bright and breezy **Seafood Bar** (☑020-670 83 55; www.theseafoodbar. com; Van Baerlestraat 5; mains €13-36; ⊘11am-11pm; ☒2/5 Van Baerlestraat) is a five-minute walk away.

Van Gogh Museum

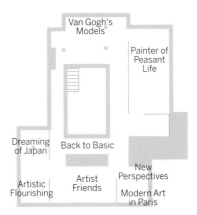

Van Gogh's Models

Painter of Peasant Life

Dreaming of Japan

Back to Basic

Artistic Flourishing

Artist Friends

New Perspectives

Modern Art in Paris

Floor 1

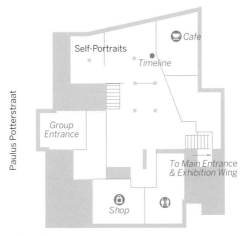

Self-Portraits

Cafe

Timeline

Paulus Potterstraat

Group Entrance

To Main Entrance & Exhibition Wing

Shop

Floor 0

intense Mediterranean light are from this period.

The Yellow House & Bedroom

Other paintings from his time in Arles include *The Yellow House* (1888), a rendering of the abode Van Gogh rented in town, intending to start an artists' colony with Gauguin. *The Bedroom* (1888) depicts Van Gogh's sleeping quarters at the house. It was in 1888 that Van Gogh sliced off part of his ear.

Wheatfield with Crows

Van Gogh had himself committed to an asylum in Saint-Rémy in 1889. While there, he painted several landscapes with cypress and olive trees, and went wild with *Irises*. In 1890 he went north to Auvers-sur-Oise. *Wheatfield with Crows* (1890), one of his last paintings, is an ominous work finished shortly before his suicide.

Extras

The museum has multiple listening stations for diverse record-ings of Van Gogh's letters, mainly to and from his closest brother Theo, who championed his work. The museum has categorised all of Van Gogh's letters online at www.vangoghletters.org. There are daily workshops (for adults and kids) where, suitably inspired, you can create your own works of art.

Other Artists

Thanks to Theo van Gogh's prescient collecting and that of the museum's curators, you'll also see works by Vincent's contemporaries, including Gauguin, Monet and Henri de Toulouse-Lautrec.

Exhibition Wing

Gerrit Rietveld, the influential Dutch architect, designed the museum's main building. Behind it, reaching towards the Museumplein, is a separate wing (opened in 1999) designed by Kisho Kurokawa and commonly referred to as 'the Mussel'. It hosts temporary exhibitions by big-name artists.

Top Experience 📷
Wander through Vondelpark

Amsterdam's favourite playground is the green expanse of Vondelpark, with its 47 hectares of lawns, ponds and winding paths receiving around 12 million visitors a year. All of Amsterdam life is here: tourists, roller skaters, dog walkers, kids and stoners. There's a constantly whizzing parade of bikes, and on sunny days you can hardly move for picnics all around the grass.

◉ MAP P112, E2

www.hetvondelpark.net

🚊 12 Van Baerlstraat, 5 Museumplein

Vondel Statue

The English-style gardens, with ponds, lawns, footbridges and winding footpaths, were laid out in 1865 and originally known as Nieuwe Park (New Park). In 1867 sculptor Louis Royer added a statue of famed poet and playwright Joost van den Vondel (1587–1679). Amsterdammers began referring to the place as Vondel's Park, which led to it being renamed.

Hippie Remnants

During the late 1960s and early 1970s, Dutch authorities turned the park into a temporary open-air dormitory for the droves of hippies who descended on Amsterdam. The sleeping bags are long gone, but remnants of the era live on in the squats that fringe the park, such as **OT301** (www.ot301.nl; Overtoom 301; 🚊1 Jan Pieter Heijestraat) and **OCCII** (📞020-671 77 78; www.occii.org; Amstelveenseweg 134; ⏰hours vary; 🚊2 Amstelveenseweg), now both legalised into underground cultural centres.

Gardens & Grounds

The park's 47 hectares encourage visitors to get out and explore. The rose garden, with some 70 different species, was added in 1936. It's in the middle of the park; signs point the way. The park also shelters several cafes, playgrounds and a wonderful outdoor **theatre** (pictured; Open-Air Theatre; 📞020-428 33 60; www.openlucht theater.nl; Vondelpark 5a; ⏰early May–early Sep; 🚊1/3/11 1e Constantijn Huygensstraat).

Picasso Sculpture

Art is strewn throughout the park, with 69 sculptures dotted throughout the leafy environs. Among them is Picasso's soaring abstract work *Figure découpée l'Oiseau (The Bird)*, better known locally as *The Fish* (1965), which he donated for the park's centenary.

★ Top Tips

o It's great to glide around and explore the park by bike. Take yours there or hire one nearby.

o Sunday is fun day at Vondelpark, when there's almost a festival atmosphere on sunny days.

o Look out for events at the park's open-air theatre during summer.

✗ Take a Break

The elegant cake-stand architecture of **Proeflokaal Brouwerij 't IJ 't Blauwe Theehuis** (www.brouwerijhetij.nl; Vondelpark 5; ⏰9am–midnight; 🛜; 🚊2 Jacob Obrechtstraat) makes for an excellent spot to sip craft beer on its inviting terrace.

Families will particularly love **Het Groot Melkhuis** (📞020-612 96 74; www.grootmelkhuis.nl; Vondelpark 2; ⏰10am–5pm; 🛜🚻; 🚊1 Jan Pieter Heijestraat), but this charming, rambling place in the park is a good spot for all.

Vondelpark & the South

200 m
0.1 miles

Rijksmuseum

Stadhouderskade

Diamond Museum

Museum Shop at the Museumplein

Van Gogh Museum

House of Bols

PC Hooftstr

Vossiusstr

Johannes Vermeerstr

Boerenwetering

Hobbemakade

Frans Halsstr

Ferdinand Bolstr

De Pijp

1e Jan Steenstr

Roelof Hartstr

Gerard Terborgstr

Reijnier Vinkeleskade

Noorder Amstel Kanaal

Oud Zuid

De Lairessestr

Cornelis Schuytstr

Willemsparkweg

Van Eeghenstr

Jan Willem Brouwersstr

Van Baerlestr

Nicolaas Maesstr

Frans van Mierisstr

Ruysdaelstr

Banstr

Stedelijk Museum

Hollandsche Manege

Vondelpark

Vondelstr

1e Constantijn Huygensstr

2e Constantijn Huygensstr

Bilderdijkstr

Nassaukade

Stadhouderskade

Marnixstr

Singelgracht

Max Euweplein

Blue Pepper

3e Helmersstr

1e Helmersstr

OUD WEST

De Hallen

Nicolaas Beetsstr

Kinkerstr

Borgerstr

Jacob van Lennepstr

Jacob van Lennepkanaal

Bellamystr

Baarsjesweg

Admiralengracht

Postjesweg

Marco Polostr

Paramaribostr

Overtoom

Jan Pieter Heijestr

Gerard Brandtstr

Willemparkweg

Koningslaan

Willemsparkweg

Amstelveenseweg

Restaurant Blauw

Toko Kok Kita

Sloterkade

3e Kostverlorenkade

Baarsjesweg

Hoofdweg

Van Spilbergenstr

Postjeskade

Curaçaostr

Cornelis Lelylaan

Konijnenweg

Valeriusstr

Johannes Verhulststr

Sights

Stedelijk Museum
MUSEUM

1 ⊙ MAP P112, E3

This fabulous museum houses the collection amassed by postwar curator Willem Sandberg. The ground-floor Stedelijk Base exhibition displays a rotating selection of the amazing collection's highlights, featuring works by Picasso, Matisse, Mondrian, Van Gogh, Rothko, Jeff Koons, Yves Klein, Lichtenstein, Yayoi Kusama and more, plus an exuberant Karel Appel mural. The museum also hosts excellent temporary exhibitions. The free in-depth audioguide is fantastic and there are themed guided tours; book online. Unlike other museums in the area, you seldom have to queue. (☎020-573 29 11; www.stedelijk.nl; Museumplein 10; adult/child €18.50/free; ⊙10am-6pm Sat-Thu, to 10pm Fri; 🚊2/3/5/12 Van Baerlestraat)

Hollandsche Manege
NOTABLE BUILDING

2 ⊙ MAP P112, D2

The neoclassical Hollandsche Manege is a surprise to discover just outside the Vondelpark. Entering is like stepping back in time, into a grandiose indoor riding school inspired by the famous Spanish Riding School in Vienna. Designed by AL van Gendt and built in 1882, it retains its charming horse-head facade and has a large riding arena inside. (☎020-618

09 42; www.dehollandschemanege. nl; Vondelstraat 140; adult/child €8/4; ⊙10am-5pm; 🚊1/11 1e Constantijn Huygensstraat)

Diamond Museum
MUSEUM

3 ⊙ MAP P112, E2

The extensive bling on display at the small, low-tech Diamond Museum is all clever recreations. You get a lot of background on the history of the trade and various historic sparkly crowns and jewels. Here you'll learn how Amsterdam was the globe's diamond trade epicentre for many centuries, where local Jews dominated the cutting and polishing business, and how the business moved to Antwerp after WWII following the decimation of the Jewish population here. (www.diamantmuseumamsterdam.nl; Paulus Potterstraat 8; adult/child €10/7.50; ⊙9am-5pm; 🚊2/5/12 Rijksmuseum)

House of Bols
MUSEUM

4 ⊙ MAP P112, E3

Cheesy but fun: here you undertake an hour's self-guided tour through this *jenever* (Dutch gin) museum. In the 'Hall of Taste' you'll try to differentiate between scents and flavours, while in the 'Distillery Room' you'll learn about the process of extraction. You'll learn more about the history of gin than you would think possible, and get to try shaking your own cocktail, plus drink a Bols confection of your choice at the end. (www.house ofbols.com; Paulus Potterstraat 14;

Museumplein: Culture Central

Amsterdam's most famous museums cluster around this public square, which has that Amsterdam essential: a skateboard ramp, as well as a playground and ice-skating pond (in winter). Locals and tourists mill around, everyone picnics here when the weather warms up, and there are food and craft stalls on the third Sunday of the month. Public concerts and events regularly take place here.

At the **Museum Shop at the Museumplein** (Map p112, E3; Paulus Potterstraat 1; ⏲10am-6pm; 🚃2/5/12 Rijksmuseum) you can you can buy museum tickets for Rijksmuseum, Van Gogh and Stedelijk at the ticket window here (8am to 4pm), which gives you direct access to avoid queuing at the museums. The shop also sells posters, cards and other art souvenirs from both institutions.

admission incl 1 cocktail €16, over 18yr only; ⏲1-6.30pm Sun-Thu, to 9pm Fri & Sat; 🚃2/5/12 Van Baerlestraat)

Eating

Ron Gastrobar INTERNATIONAL €€€

5 MAP P112, B4

Ron Blaauw ran his two-Michelin-star restaurant in these pared-down, spacious designer premises before turning it into a more affordable 'gastrobar' (still Michelin-starred), whereby you get the quality without the formality. He serves gourmet tapas-style dishes, dry-aged rib steaks and stellar seafood sharing dishes, or you can choose the 'best of Gastrobar' six-course menu for €69.50 per person. (☎020-496 19 43; www.rongastrobar.nl; Sophialaan 55; dishes €17.50, steak & seafood €42.50-92.50; ⏲noon-2.30pm & 5.30-10.30pm; 🛜; 🚃2 Amstelveenseweg)

Adam GASTRONOMY €€€

6 MAP P112, B3

This seriously gourmet, chic and intimate restaurant serves exquisitely presented food. The surprise menu changes on a monthly basis; choose from one of the course menus of vegetarian or meat and fish dishes. Dessert is either a cheese platter or a chef's surprise, and paired wines are available for €7.50 per glass. (☎020-233 98 52; www.restaurantadam.nl; Overtoom 515; 3-/4-/5-/6-course menus €38.50/46.50/52.50/62; ⏲6-10.30pm Tue-Sat; 🍴; 🚃1/11/17 Surinameplein)

Braai BBQ Bar BARBECUE €

7 MAP P112, A3

Once a *haringhuis* (herring stand), this tiny place is now a street-food-style barbecue bar, with a great canal-side setting. Braai's speciality is marinated,

barbecued ribs (half or full rack), biltong and roasted sausages, but there is a veggie burger, too. Tables scatter under the trees alongside the water. No alcohol is served. (📞020-221 13 76; www.braaiamsterdam.nl; Schinkelhavenkade 1; dishes €6.50-15.50; ⏰4-9.30pm; 🚊1/11/17 Surinameplein)

Alchemist Garden VEGAN €

8 ✕ MAP P112, B3

This bright, high-ceilinged cafe's food may be gluten-, lactose- and glucose-free, but it's certainly tasty. There's a health-rich, vitamin-filled organic menu (raw 'hot dog', pumpkin burger and pesto-stuffed portobello mushrooms), plus smoothies, juices, a huge range of herbal teas, organic wine by the bottle and guilt-free treats such as raw chocolate cake. Many ingredients are from the owner's own garden. (📞020-334 33 35; www.facebook.com/AlchemistGarden; Overtoom 409; dishes €4-13; ⏰9am-10pm Mon-Sat, noon-9pm Sun; 🌿; 🚊1/11 Rhijnvis Feithstraat)

Van 't Spit ROTISSERIE €€

9 ✕ MAP P112, C1

At stripped-back Van 't Spit it's all about roast chicken, with piles of wood ready for the rotisserie. Choices are simple – select from a half or whole chicken (there are no other mains), and decide if you want sides (corn on the cob, fries, salad and homemade coleslaw).

Alchemist Garden

Indonesian Cuisine

The Netherlands' historical ties with Indonesia mean there are plenty of places to try its cuisines.

The most famous Indonesian dish is a *rijsttafel* (Indonesian banquet): a dozen or more tiny dishes such as braised beef, pork satay and ribs served with white rice. Other popular dishes are *nasi goreng* – fried rice with onion, pork, shrimp and spices, often topped with a fried egg or shredded omelette – and *bami goreng*, which is the same thing but with noodles in place of rice. Indonesian food is usually served mild for Western palates. If you want it hot (*pedis*, pronounced 'p-dis'), say so, but be prepared for the ride of a lifetime.

Top Indonesian dining addresses near the Vondelpark include **Restaurant Blauw** (Map p112, A4; ☎ 020-675 50 00; www.restaurant blauw.nl; Amstelveenseweg 158; mains €22.50-27.50, rijsttafel per person €30-35; ⏱ 6-10pm Mon-Fri, 5pm-10pm Sat & Sun; 🚊 2 Amstelveenseweg), which offers meat, seafood or vegetarian *rijsttafel* feasts; **Blue Pepper** (Map p112, D1; ☎ 020-489 70 39; www.restaurantbluepepper. com; Nassaukade 366; mains €18-20, rijsttafel per person from €44.50; ⏱ 5.30-10pm; 🚶; 🚊 7/10 Raamplein), one of Amsterdam's finest gourmet Indonesian restaurants; and **Toko Kok Kita** (Map p112, A4; ☎ 020-670 29 33; www.kokkita.nl; Amstelveenseweg 166; mains €5-9; ⏱ noon-8.30pm Tue-Sat, from 5pm Sun; 🚊 2 Amstelveenseweg), a humble Indonesian *toko* (shop) attracting queues for its bargain-priced Indonesian dishes.

(www.vantspit.nl; De Clercqstraat 95; half/whole chicken €11.90/23; ⏱ kitchen 5-10pm, bar to 1am; 🚊 13/19 Willem de Zwijgerlaan)

l'Entrecôte et les Dames

FRENCH €€

10 🍴 MAP P112, E3

Black-and-white awnings, a wall made from wooden drawers and a wrought-iron balcony set the scene at this restaurant, which has a simple menu of steak or fish. Go for the *entrecôte* (premium beef steak) at dinner or a steak sandwich for lunch, and save room for scrumptious desserts: perhaps chocolate mousse, *tarte au citron* (lemon tart) or *crêpes au Grand Marnier*. (☎ 020-679 88 88; www.entrecote-et-les-dames.nl; Van Baerlestraat 47-49; lunch mains €14.50, 2-course dinner

menu €25.75; ⏱noon-3pm & 5.30-10pm; 🚋3/5/12 Museumplein)

Drinking

Labyrinth   COCKTAIL BAR

11 🚇 MAP P112, A4

Mixologist Sam Kingue Ebelle concocts impressively inventive cocktails (€10.50 to €13) at this moody bar on Amstelveenseweg. For theatrical drama, try the Full Severity of Compassion (rye whisky, spiced rum, cherry brandy, vermouth infused with cocoa nibs, absinthe and bitters), delivered in a box and wafting gum-arabic smoke when opened. (📞020-845 09 72; www.labyrinth amsterdam.nl; Amstelveenseweg 53; ⏱4.30pm-midnight Mon, Wed, Thu & Sun, to 2am Fri & Sat)

Lot Sixty One   COFFEE

12 🚇 MAP P112, C1

Look downstairs to the open cellar to see (and, better still, smell) fresh coffee beans being roasted on the Probat at this streetwise spot. Beans are sourced through distributors from individual eco-friendly farms in Brazil, Kenya and Rwanda, to name a few. All coffees are double shots (unless you specify otherwise); watch Kinkerstraat's passing parade from a window seat. (www.lotsixtyonecoffee.com; Kinkerstraat 112; ⏱8am-6pm Mon-Fri, 9am-6pm Sat & Sun; 🛜; 🚋3/7/17 Bilderdijkstraat)

Edel   BAR

13 🚇 MAP P112, B1

On Het Sieraard's waterfront, Edel has lots of waterside seating as it's at the sweet spot where two canals cross. Inside and out it's filled with creative types who work in the local buildings. With hipster staff and creative food on offer, it really comes into its own in summer, lit by a canopy of twinkling fairy lights after dark. (📞020-799 50 00; www.lokaaledel.nl; Postjesweg 1; ⏱noon-midnight; 🚋7/17 Witte de Withstraat)

Butcher's Tears   BREWERY

14 🚇 MAP P112, A4

In-the-know hop heads like to go straight to the source of cult brewers Butcher's Tears. The brewery's all-white clinical-feeling taproom is tucked at the end of an out-of-the-way industrial alley and offers a rotating line-up of beers on tap, drawing inspiration from historical brewing techniques. You can pull up a chair in the front car park on sunny days. (www.butchers-tears.com; Karperweg 45; ⏱4-9pm Wed-Sun; 🚋24 Haarlemmermeerstation)

Golden Brown Bar   BAR

15 🚇 MAP P112, C2

This perennially hip, two-level bar attracts a young professional crowd that spills out onto the pavement. It does great cocktails and doubles as a Thai restaurant. (www.goldenbrownbar.nl; Jan Pieter Heijestraat 146; ⏱11am-1am Sun-Thu,

to 3am Fri & Sat; 📶; 🚊1 Jan Pieter Heijestraat)

Entertainment

Concertgebouw   CLASSICAL MUSIC

16 ⭐ MAP P112, E3

The Concert Hall was built in 1888 by AL van Gendt, who managed to engineer its near-perfect acoustics. Bernard Haitink, former conductor of the Royal Concertgebouw Orchestra, remarked that the world-famous hall was the orchestra's best instrument. Free half-hour concerts take place Wednesdays at 12.30pm from September to June; arrive early. Try the Last Minute Ticket Shop (www.lastminuteticketshop.nl) for half-price seats to selected performances. (Concert Hall; 📞020-671 83 45; www.concertgebouw.nl; Concertgebouwplein 10; 🕓box office 1-7pm Mon-Fri, 10am-7pm Sat & Sun; 🚊3/5/12 Museumplein)

Shopping

Pied à Terre   BOOKS

17 🅐 MAP P112, D2

Travel lovers will be in heaven in the galleried, skylit interior of Europe's largest travel bookshop. If it's travel- or outdoor-related, you can dream over it here: gorgeous globes, travel guides in multiple languages and over 600,000 maps. Order a coffee, pull up a chair and plan your next trip. (📞020-627 44 55; www.piedaterre.nl; Overtoom 135-137; 🕓1-6pm Mon, 10am-6pm Tue, Wed & Sat, to 7pm Thu & Fri; 🚊1/3/11 1e Constantijn Huygensstraat)

J&B Craft Drinks   DRINKS

18 🅐 MAP P112, C2

J&B Craft Drinks offers a huge range of craft beers, ciders and tasty soda from all over the globe, which are available cold from the fridge, making them perfect to take to the nearby Vondelpark on a hot day. (📞020-244 01 77; www.facebook.com/jbcraftdrinks; Jan Pieter Heijestraat 148; 🕓2-8pm Tue-Thu & Sun, noon-10pm Fri, to 9pm Sat; 🚊1/11 Jan Pieter Heijestraat)

VLVT

CLAIRE BISSELL / LONELY PLANET ©

De Hallen
Cultural Complex

These red-brick 1902-built tram sheds were formerly used as a squat before being turned into this breathtaking skylit space. **De Hallen** (Map p112, C1; www.dehallen-amsterdam.nl; Bellamyplein 51; 🚋7/17 Ten Katestraat) was stunningly converted in 2014 to create a cultural complex incorporating a **food hall** (www.foodhallen.nl; De Hallen, Hannie Dankbaar Passage 3; dishes €3-20; ⏱11am-11.30pm Sun-Thu, to 1am Fri & Sat; 🚋7/17 Ten Katestraat), a brasserie, a library, design shops such as the **Denim City Store** (📞020-820 86 14; www.denimcity.org; De Hallen, Hannie Dankbaar Passage 22; ⏱11am-6pm Mon-Fri, 10am-6pm Sat, noon-5pm Sun; 🚋7/17 Ten Katestraat) and the **Maker Store** (📞020-261 76 67; www.themakerstore.nl; De Hallen, Hannie Dankbaar Passage 39; ⏱noon-7pm Tue-Fri & Sun, from 11am Sat; 🚋7/17 Ten Katestraat), a **bike seller-repairer** (📞020-489 70 29; www.recyclefietsen.nl; De Hallen, Hannie Dankbaar Passage 27; ⏱noon-6pm Mon, 11am-7pm Tue-Fri, 11am-6pm Sat & Sun; 🚋7/17 Ten Katestraat), a **cinema** (www.filmhallen.nl; De Hallen, Hannie Dankbaar Passage 12; tickets adult/child from €11.50/8; 🚋7/17 Ten Katestraat) and a hotel. Regular events held inside include themed weekend markets (such as organic produce or Dutch design).

A lively daily (except Sunday) street market, **Ten Katemarkt** (Ten Katestraat; ⏱9am-5pm Mon-Sat; 🚋7/17 Ten Katestraat), takes place outside.

VLVT
FASHION & ACCESSORIES

19 🔒 MAP P112, D4

Up-and-coming Dutch-designed fashion for women is stocked at this chic, light-filled boutique, featuring carefully curated Dutch and international designers, including labels such as Elisabetta Franchi, Notes du Nord, Pierre Balmain and Zoe Karssen. (www.vlvt.nl; Cornelis Schuytstraat 22; ⏱10am-6pm Tue-Sat, noon-6pm Sun & Mon; 🚋2 Cornelis Schuytstraat)

De Winkel van Nijntje
TOYS

20 🔒 MAP P112, F4

A Miffy (Nijntje in Dutch) emporium, devoted entirely to the much-adored character of Dutch illustrator Dick Bruna. The mouthless one is celebrated in all sorts of enticing merchandise, from crocheted dolls to Royal Delftware plates. (www.dewinkelvannijntje.nl; Scheldestraat 61; ⏱1-6pm Mon, 10am-6pm Tue-Fri, to 5pm Sat, noon-5pm Sun; ♿; 🚋12 Scheldestraat)

Explore
De Pijp

A hotbed of creativity, multicultural De Pijp is less than five minutes from Centraal Station by metro yet preserves its village-like atmosphere. The neighbourhood's centrepiece is Amsterdam's largest street market, the colourful Albert Cuypmarkt, and the fashion boutiques, vintage shops, experimental restaurants and free-spirited cafés (pubs) that surround it.

The Short List

◦ **Albert Cuypmarkt (p123)** *Feasting your senses at Amsterdam's biggest street market.*

◦ **Sarphatipark (p123)** *Strolling through an urban oasis of lawns, statues, ponds.*

◦ **Boaty (p125)** *Setting sail in an electric boat to cruise Amsterdam's canals.*

◦ **Heineken Experience (p125)** *Touring the boisterously fun brewery before boarding its canal boat for a cruise across town to A'DAM Tower.*

◦ **Bakers & Roasters (p128)** *Delving into De Pijp's thriving brunch scene at specialists such as Bakers & Roasters.*

Getting There & Around

Ⓜ The Noord/Zuidlijn (north–south metro line; M52) serves De Pijp station.

🚊 Tram 24 rolls to/from Centraal Station along Ferdinand Bolstraat. Tram 4 travels from Centraal via Rembrandtplein to De Pijp. Tram 3 traverses De Pijp between the Vondelpark and Oost. Tram 12 cuts through De Pijp en route from Leidseplein to the south.

Neighbourhood Map on p124

Heineken Experience (p125) ANTON_IVANOV/SHUTTERSTOCK ©

Walking Tour 🥾

Discovering Bohemian De Pijp

Artists and intellectuals have hung out in De Pijp since the 19th century, when the former slum's cheap housing drew them in. The district still wafts bohemian flair, from the spicy market at its epicentre to the cool-cat cafes and retro shops that jam its streets. A surprise red-light area also makes an appearance.

Walk Facts

Start Albert Cuypmarkt
End Barça
Length 1.7km; three hours

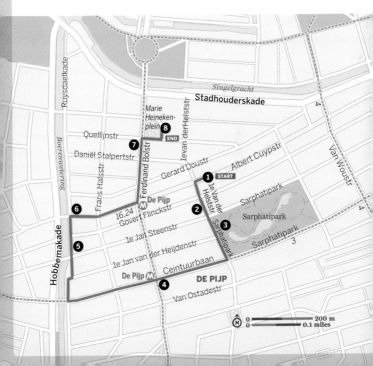

❶ Albert Cuypmarkt

The 650m-long **Albert Cuypmarkt** (www.albertcuyp-markt.amsterdam; Albert Cuypstraat, btwn Ferdinand Bolstraat & Van Woustraat; ⏱9am-5pm Mon-Sat; Ⓜ De Pijp, 🚊24 Marie Heinekenplein) is Amsterdam's largest and busiest market. Vendors loudly tout their gadgets, clothing and spices, while Dutch snack stalls tempt with herring sandwiches and caramel-syrup-filled *stroopwafels*.

❷ Katsu

De Pijp's favourite coffeeshop (cannabis cafe), **Katsu** (www.katsu. nl; 1e Van Der Helststraat 70; ⏱10am-midnight Mon-Thu, to 1am Fri & Sat, 11am-midnight Sun; Ⓜ De Pijp, 🚊3 2e Van der Helststraat), is always filled with colourful characters.

❸ Sarphatipark

The Vondelpark might be bigger in size and reputation, but **Sarphatipark** (Sarphatipark; 🚊3 2e Van der Helststraat) offers pastoral relaxation with fewer crowds. In the centre you'll see a bombastic temple with a fountain, gargoyles and a bust of Samuel Sarphati (1813–66), a Jewish doctor, businessman and urban innovator.

❹ CT Coffee & Coconuts

CT Coffee & Coconuts (📞020-354 11 04; www.coffeeandcoconuts. com; Ceintuurbaan 282-284; mains lunch €8-15.50, dinner €15-19; ⏱8am-11pm; 🛜; Ⓜ De Pijp, 🚊3/12/24 De Pijp) spreads through a cathedral-like building that was a 1920s cinema. It's especially popular for brunch dishes like coconut, almond and buckwheat pancakes.

❺ Red-light Area

As you walk along Ruysdaelkade between 1e Jan Steenstraat and Albert Cuypstraat, you'll be greeted by the unexpected sight of a strip of **red-light windows**, minus the stag parties and drunken crowds that prowl the main Red Light District in the city centre.

❻ Café Binnen Buiten

The minute there's a sliver of sunshine, **Café Binnen Buiten** (www. cafebinnenbuiten.nl; Ruysdaelkade 115; ⏱10am-1am Sun-Thu, to 3am Fri & Sat; 🛜; Ⓜ De Pijp, 🚊3/12/24 De Pijp) gets packed, particularly its canal-side terrace.

❼ Record Mania

The wonderfully retro **Record Mania** (www.recordmania.nl; Ferdinand Bolstraat 30; ⏱10am-6pm Mon-Sat, noon-6pm Sun; 🚊24 Marie Heinekenplein) is where neighbourhood folks go for their vinyl and CDs. The shop, with old posters, stained-glass windows, and records and CDs embedded in the floor, is a treasure in itself.

❽ Barça

Buzzing bar **Barça** (www.barca.nl; Marie Heinekenplein 30-31; ⏱11am-midnight Sun-Thu, to 2am Fri & Sat; 🛜; 🚊24 Marie Heinekenplein) is the heartbeat of Marie Heinekenplein. Hang out in the plush gold-and-dark-timber interior or spread out on the terrace.

De Pijp

1
2
3
4

Ruyschstraat
1e Ooster-parkstr
Weesperzijde
Amstel
Weesperzijde
Amsteldijk

For reviews see

😊	Sights	p125
🍽	Eating	p126
🍷	Drinking	p129
🎭	Entertainment	p131
🛍	Shopping	p131

200 m
0.1 miles

Amsteldijk
Amsteldijk

Ruysschstr
Hemonystraat
Hemonylaan
Govert Flinckstr
2e Jan Steenstr
2e Jan van der Heijdenstr
Sint-Willibrordusstr
Van Woustr
Ceintuurbaan
Rustenburgerstr
Van Ostadestr
Van Woustr

Tolstr
Tellegenstr

9
20
13
15
5

Little
Collins
1e Sweelinckstr
Sarphatipark
Sarphatipark
Sarphatipark
Sarphatipark

De
Dageraad
Pieter Lodewijk
Takstr
Burgemeester

3

Stadhouderskade
Singelgracht
2e Jacob van Campenstr
Gerard Doustr
Ajax Bike
Albert Cuypstr
1e Van der Helststr
Karel du Jardinstr
DE PIJP
Lutmastr
Rustenburgerstr
Van Ostadestr
2e Van der Helststr
Café
Ruis

22
7
18
21
19
12
6

Van der
Helstplein

Marie
Heineken
Experience
Hameken
1e Van der Helstr
Scandinavian
Embassy
Volendammer
Vishandel
De Pijp
Ferdinand Bolstr
Van der Helstplein

Boaty
16
2

1
24
23
11
8

Bakers &
Roasters
Quellijnstr
1e Jacob
van Campenstr
Daniël Stalpertstr
Frans Halsstr
Govert Flinckstr
1e Jan Steenstr
1e Jan van der Heijdenstr
Ceintuurbaan
De Pijp
Van Ostadestr
Rustenburgerstr
Cornelis Trooststr
Van Hilligaertstr
Jozef Israëlskade

17
10
4
14

12

Honthorststr
1e Jacob
van Campenstr
Ruysdaelkade
Boerenwetering
Ruysdaelkade
Ruysdaelkade
Cornelis Anthoniszstr
Roelof Hartstr
Hobbemakade
Hobbemakade
Harmoniehof
Stadionweg

25

3, 12, 24

Sights

Heineken Experience   BREWERY

1 ◉ MAP P124, B1

On the site of the company's former brewery, Heineken's self-guided 'Experience' provides an entertaining overview of the brewing process, with a multimedia exhibit where you 'become' a beer by getting shaken up, sprayed with water and subjected to heat. Prebooking tickets online saves adults €3 and, crucially, allows you to skip the ticket queues. Guided 2½-hour VIP tours end with a five-beer tasting and cheese pairing. Great-value Rock the City tickets include a 45-minute canal cruise to A'DAM Tower (p167). (📞020-523 94 35; https://tickets.heinekenexperience. com; Stadhouderskade 78; adult/ child self-guided tour €21/14.50, VIP guided tour €55, Rock the City ticket €32.50; ⏰10.30am-9pm daily Jul & Aug, 10.30am-7.30pm Mon-Thu, to 9pm Fri-Sun Sep-Jun; Ⓜ️Vijzelgracht, 🚊24 Marie Heinekenplein)

Boaty   BOATING

2 ◉ MAP P124, C4

Boaty's location on the peaceful Amstelkanaal makes it an ideal launching pad for exploring the waterways before approaching the crowded city-centre canals. Rental includes a map outlining suggested routes; you don't need a boat licence or prior experience. Book ahead online, or phone for same-day reservations. Its eco-friendly electric boats carry up to six people. (📞06 2714 9493; www.amsterdamrentaboat.com; Jozef Israëlskade; boat rental per 3hr/full day from €79/179; ⏰9am-30min before sunset early Mar-Oct; 🚊4/12 Scheldestraat)

Holland or the Netherlands?

'Holland' is a popular synonym for the Netherlands, yet it only refers to the combined provinces of Noord (North) and Zuid (South) Holland. (Amsterdam is Noord-Holland's largest city; Haarlem is the provincial capital.) The rest of the country is not Holland, even if locals themselves often make the mistake.

De Dageraad   ARCHITECTURE

3 ◉ MAP P124, D4

Following the key Housing Act of 1901, which forced the city to rethink neighbourhood planning and condemn slums, De Dageraad housing estate was developed between 1918 and 1923 for poorer families. One of the most original architects of the expressionist Amsterdam School, Piet Kramer, drew up plans for this idiosyncratic complex in collaboration with Michel de Klerk. (Dawn Housing Project; Pieter Lodewijk Takstraat; 🚊4 Amstelkade)

Eating

Avocado Show

CAFE €€

4 MAP P124, B1

A world first, this cafe uses avocado in *every* dish, often in ingeniously functional ways (burgers with avocado halves instead of buns, salad 'bowls' made from avocado slices). Finish with avocado ice cream or sorbet. Avocado cocktails include a spicy Guaco Mary and an avocado daiquiri. It doesn't take reservations, so prepare to queue. Cards only; no cash. (www.theavocadoshow.com; Daniël Stalpertstraat 61; mains €10-16; ☉9am-5pm; 🛜🖋; Ⓜ De Pijp, 🚊24 Marie Heinekenplein)

Graham's Kitchen

GASTRONOMY €€€

5 MAP P124, E1

A veteran of Michelin-starred kitchens, chef Graham Mee now crafts intricate dishes at his own premises. Multicourse menus (no à la carte) might include a venison and crispy smoked-beetroot macaron, cucumber and gin-cured salmon, veal with wasabi and ghost crab, and deconstructed summer-berry crumble with wood-calamint ice cream. Mee personally explains each dish to diners. (📞020-364 25 60; www.grahamskitchen.amsterdam; Hemonystraat 38; 3-/4-/5-/6-course menus €39/49/59/68; ☉6-10pm Tue-Sat; 🚊4 Stadhouderskade)

De Pijp Eating

Broodje haring (herring roll)

RICHARD NEBESKY/LONELY PLANET ©

How to Eat a Herring

'Hollandse Nieuwe' isn't a fashion trend – it's the fresh catch of super-tasty herring, raked in every June. Vendors sell the salty fish all over town. Although Dutch tradition calls for dangling the herring above your mouth, in Amsterdam the fish is served chopped in bite-size chunks and eaten with a toothpick, topped with *uitjes* (diced onions) and *zuur* (sweet pickles). A *broodje haring* (herring roll) is even handier, as the fluffy white roll holds on the toppings and keeps your fingers clean.

Locals flock for a herring fix at **Volendammer Vishandel** (Map p124, C2; 1e Van der Helststraat; dishes €2-6; 8am-5pm Mon-Sat; De Pijp, 24 24 Marie Heinekenplein), which has its own fishing fleet.

Sir Hummus
MIDDLE EASTERN €

6 MAP P124, C3

Sir Hummus is the brainchild of three young Israelis whose passion for the chickpea dip led to a London street-market stall and then this hummus-dedicated cafe. Creamy, all-natural, preservative- and additive-free hummus is served with pillowy pita bread and salad; SH also makes fantastic falafels. You can eat in or take away, but arrive early before it sells out. (www.sirhummus.nl; Van der Helstplein 2; dishes €7-13; noon-9pm Wed-Sun; 3/4 2e Van der Helststraat)

Le Salonard
DELI €

7 MAP P124, C1

Piled high with pastries (both savoury – such as quiches and gourmet sandwiches and sausage rolls – and sweet, including custard tarts and moelleux chocolate cakes), cheeses, charcuterie, breads and a floor-to-ceiling wall of wines, this enticing deli also makes up *borrel* (drinks) platters to snack on over vintages by the bottle or glass on the pavement terrace out front. (www.lesalonard.com; 1e Van der Helststraat 21; dishes €4.50-9.50; 10am-4pm Mon, to 6pm Tue-Sat; 24 Marie Heinekenplein)

Sugo
PIZZA €

8 MAP P124, B3

Spectacular pizza slices at this two-storey restaurant are cooked daily, displayed beneath glass and warmed in ovens. Its 20 different topping combinations include caramelised onion, mascarpone, walnut and black olive, or potato, mushroom and truffles. Veggies are locally sourced; meats and cheeses are from small farms in Italy. Takeaway packaging is made from recycled paper and energy is 100% sustainable. (www.sugopizza.nl; Ferdinand Bolstraat 107; pizza slice €4-5.50; 11am-9pm Sun-Thu, to 10pm Fri & Sat; De Pijp, 3/12/24 De Pijp)

Brunch in De Pijp

De Pijp is at the epicentre of Amsterdam's brunch scene. Top picks:

Bakers & Roasters (Map p124, B1; www.bakersandroasters.com; 1e Jacob van Campenstraat 54; dishes €9-16.50; �8.30am-4pm; 🛜; 🚃24 Marie Heinekenplein) Sumptuous brunch dishes at Bakers & Roasters include banana-nutbread French toast with homemade banana marmalade and crispy bacon; Navajo eggs with pulled pork, avocado, mango salsa and chipotle cream; and a smoked-salmon stack with poached eggs, potato cakes and hollandaise. Wash them down with a fiery Bloody Mary.

Scandinavian Embassy (Map p124, C2; www.scandinavianembassy.nl; Sarphatipark 34; dishes €5-14; �8am-6pm Mon-Fri, 9am-6pm Sat & Sun; 🚃3/4 2e Van der Helststraat) Porridge with blueberries, honey and coconut, served with goat's-milk yoghurt; salt-cured salmon on Danish rye; and freshly baked cinnamon buns make this blond-wood-panelled spot a perfect place to start the day – as does its coffee sourced from Scandinavian microroasteries.

Little Collins (Map p124, D1; 📞 020-753 96 36; www.littlecollins.nl; 1e Sweelinckstraat 19; tapas €4-16, brunch €8-16; �9am-4pm Mon & Tue, to 10pm Wed-Sun; 🛜; 🚃3/4 Van Woustraat) Brunch dishes at this hip hang-out might include toasted brioche with grilled halloumi, homemade plum jam, crème fraîche, hazelnuts, basil and mint. The evening tapas menu is equally inspired.

Geflipt
BURGERS €

 9 ✖ MAP P124, D1

Competition is fierce for the best burgers in this food-driven neighbourhood, but Geflipt is a serious contender. In a stripped-back, industrial-chic interior, it serves luscious combinations (such as Gasconne beef, bacon, golden cheddar, red-onion compote and fried egg) on brioche buns with sauces cooked daily on the premises from locally sourced ingredients. (www.gefliptburgers.nl; Van Woustraat 15;

dishes €9-13; �11.30am-9.30pm Sun-Thu, to 10.30pm Fri & Sat; 🛜; 🚃4 Stadhouderskade)

Spang Makandra
SURINAMESE €

10 ✖ MAP P124, B2

There are just 26 seats at this cosy restaurant, and it's a red-hot favourite with students and Surinamese and Indonesian expats; you'll need to book for dinner. The reward is a fabulous array of dishes including fish soups and satay with spicy sauces at astonishingly cheap prices. All the food is halal;

no alcohol is served. (☎020-670 50 81; www.spangmakandra.nl; Gerard Doustraat 39; mains €6-12; ⏰11am-10pm Mon-Sat, 1-10pm Sun; Ⓜ De Pijp, 🚊24 Marie Heinekenplein)

Butcher

BURGERS €

11 ❌ MAP P124, C2

Burgers at this sizzling spot are cooked right in front of you (behind a glass screen, so you won't get splattered). Mouthwatering choices include Silence of the Lamb (with spices and tahini), the Codfather (beer-battered blue cod and homemade tartar sauce), an Angus-beef truffle burger and a veggie version. Ask about its 'secret kitchen' cocktail bar. (☎020-470 78 75; www.the-butcher. com; Albert Cuypstraat 129; burgers €7-13.50; ⏰11am-midnight; Ⓜ De Pijp, 🚊24 Marie Heinekenplein)

Massimo

GELATO €

12 ❌ MAP P124, C3

Gelato is made daily on-site from family recipes using local, organic milk, butter and yoghurt, along with imported Italian ingredients such as lemons from the passionate fourth-generation gelato maker's native Liguria. Scrumptious flavours including cinnamon and fig; honey, yoghurt and cherry; coffee and hazelnut; and pear and walnut are scooped with a spatula into hand-rolled waffle cones or tubs. Cards only. (Van Ostadestraat 147; 1/2/3/4 scoops €1.60/3.20/4.50/6; ⏰1-10pm; 🚊3/4 2e Van der Helststraat)

Bar Fisk

SEAFOOD €€

13 ❌ MAP P124, D2

Fish-scale tiles in marine blues and greens clad the bar at switched-on seafood bar Fisk. Small lunchtime sharing plates (oysters with limoncello dressing; Zeeland mussels steamed in vanilla and white wine) precede more substantial dinner mains such as barbecued whole sea bass with fennel pesto. (☎020-235 21 17; www.barfisk.nl; 1e Sweelinckstraat 23; mains lunch €8-12, dinner €12.50-18.50; ⏰kitchen 6-10pm Mon-Wed, 5-10pm Thu & Fri, noon-10pm Sat & Sun, bar to 1am; 🛜; 🚊3/4 Van Woustraat)

Drinking

Brouwerij Troost

BREWERY

14 🍺 MAP P124, B3

Watch beer being brewed in copper vats behind a glass wall at this outstanding craft brewery. Its dozen beers include a summery blonde, a smoked porter, a strong tripel and a deep-red Imperial IPA; it also distils cucumber and juniper gin from its beer, and serves fantastic bar food, including crispy prawn tacos and humongous burgers. Book on weekend evenings. (☎020-760 58 20; www.brouwerijtroost.nl; Cornelis Troostplein 21; ⏰4pm-midnight Mon-Thu, 4pm-3am Fri, 2pm-3am Sat, 2pm-midnight Sun; 🛜; 🚊4/12 Cornelis Troostplein)

Rayleigh & Ramsay

WINE BAR

15 🍺 MAP P124, E2

Wine is a serious business at this vintage-style bar named for

Local Hangouts

Many successful Amsterdam businesses put down their first roots in De Pijp, and this innovative neighbourhood has a constant turnover of pop-ups, startups and new openings. Backstreets to watch include Frans Halsstraat, 1e Van der Helststraat, 2e Van der Helststraat, Cornelis Troostplein and Ruysdaelkade.

Tucked-away square Van der Helstplein is lined with low-key local *cafés* such as **Café Ruis** (Map p124, C3; www.cafe-ruis.nl; Van der Helstplein 9; ⏰3pm-1am Mon-Thu, to 3am Fri, noon-3am Sat, to 1am Sun; 📶; 🚋3/4 2e Van der Helststraat).

the two Scottish chemists who discovered that oxygen is lighter than argon gas, which R&R uses to prevent oxidisation. Its top-up-card payment system lets you dispense wines yourself by the 'sip', half or full glass. Alongside cheese and charcuterie, sharing platters feature shucked oysters, tinned sardines and shrimp croquettes. (www.rr.wine; Van Woustraat 97; ⏰3pm-1am Mon-Thu, noon-2am Fri & Sat, noon-1am Sun; 🚋3/4 Van Woustraat)

Twenty Third Bar   COCKTAIL BAR

16 📍 MAP P124, C4

High up in the skyscraping Hotel Okura Amsterdam (p133), Twenty Third Bar has sweeping views to the west and south. The adjacent twin-Michelin-starred kitchen of **Ciel Bleu** (📞020-678 74 50; www.cielbleu.nl; tasting menus from €195; ⏰6.30-10pm Mon-Sat) also creates stunning bar snacks (€9 to €15) such as tuna sashimi cornets or goose liver and mango macarons, as well as syrups, purées and infusions for its cocktails; champagne cocktails are a speciality. (www.okura.nl; Hotel Okura Amsterdam, Ferdinand Bolstraat 333; ⏰6pm-1am Sun-Thu, to 2am Fri & Sat; 🚋4/12 Cornelius Troostplein)

Jacob's Juice   JUICE BAR

17 📍 MAP P124, B1

Reducing food waste was the inspiration behind Jacob's Juice. Its owners collect imperfect fruit and vegetables each day from the Albert Cuypmarkt that stallholders would otherwise discard (an average of 500kg per month). They then transform them into super-healthy juices (such as cucumber, celery and lemon), smoothies (eg pineapple, raspberry and passion fruit) and pickled veggies in recycled jam jars. (www.jacobs-juice.com; 1e Jacob Van Campenstraat 34; ⏰9am-5pm Mon & Wed-Sat, 10am-5pm Sun; 🚋24 Marie Heinekenplein)

Boca's   BAR

18 📍 MAP P124, C2

Boca's (inspired by the Italian word for 'mouth') is the ultimate spot for *borrel* (drinks). Mezzanine seating overlooks the cushion-

strewn interior, but in summer the best seats are on the terrace facing leafy Sarphatipark. Its pared-down wine list (seven by-the-glass choices) goes perfectly with sharing platters (fish, cheese, meat or vegetarian). (www.bar-bocas.nl; Sarphatipark 4; ⏰noon-1am Mon-Thu, 10am-3am Fri & Sat, 11am-1am Sun; 📶; 🚊3/4 2e Van der Helststraat)

Entertainment

Rialto Cinema
CINEMA

19 ⭐ MAP P124, C3

Opened in 1920, this art deco cinema near Sarphatipark shows eclectic art-house fare from around the world (foreign films have Dutch subtitles). Tickets can be purchased online or at the box office. There are three screens and a stylish on-site cafe. (📞020-676 87 00; www.rialtofilm.nl; Ceintuurbaan 338; adult/child from €11/7; ⏰noon-midnight; 🚊3/4 2e Van der Helststraat)

Shopping

Hutspot
DESIGN

20 🔒 MAP P124, D1

Named after the Dutch dish of boiled and mashed veggies, 'Hotchpotch' was founded with a mission to give young entrepreneurs the chance to sell their work. As a result, this concept store is an inspired mishmash of Dutch-designed furniture, furnishings, art, homewares and clothing as well as an in-house cafe, a barber, a photo booth and various pop-ups. (www.hutspot.com; Van Woustraat

Rialto Cinema

4; ⊙10am-7pm Mon-Sat, noon-6pm Sun; 🛜; 🚊4 Stadhouderskade)

Cottoncake CONCEPT STORE

21 🔒 MAP P124, C2

Painted cotton-white inside and out, this chic little shop makes and sells its own scented candles and perfumes, and stocks fashion, jewellery and homewares from Dutch designers Yaya and Mimi et Toi as well as international labels. It has a small cafe on its mezzanine where you can stop for homemade cakes, waffles, fresh-squeezed juices and Amsterdam White Label coffee. (www.cottoncake.nl; 1e Van der Helststraat 76; ⊙10am-6.30pm Mon-Fri, to 6pm Sat, 11am-6pm Sun; 🚊3/4 2e Van der Helststraat)

Bier Baum DRINKS

22 🔒 MAP P124, C2

Perfect for Sarphatipark picnic supplies, Bier Baum has fridges keeping many of its craft beers cold, and growlers that you can fill by the litre. Look out for Dutch brews such as Amsterdam's Brouwerij 't IJ, Haarlem's Uitje Brewing Co and Nijmegen's Oersoep, and international beers from as far afield as New Zealand and Hawaii. (www.bier-baum.nl; Sarphatipark 1; ⊙2-10pm Sun-Fri, noon-10pm Sat; 🚊3/4 2e Van der Helststraat)

Brick Lane FASHION & ACCESSORIES

23 🔒 MAP P124, B2

Individual, affordable designs for women arrive at this London-

De Pijp Shopping

King's Day celebrations

MELANIE LEMAHIEU/SHUTTERSTOCK ©

The Netherlands' Largest Barometer

Rising 75m above low-rise Amsterdam, the landmark **Hotel Okura Amsterdam** (☎020-678 71 11; www.okura.nl; Ferdinand Bolstraat 333; @ 🛜; 🚊4/12 Cornelis Troostplein) building is visible from afar both day and evening. Each night the roof's perimeter is illuminated by LED lights, which change colour depending on the barometer's reading for the following day. Blue lights mean a bright, sunny day is forecast. Green lights mean bad weather is on the way. 'White' (more like a pale-pinkish colour, and the most common) means the weather will be changeable.

The lights also change colour on special occasions, producing a variegated rainbow effect for **Pride Amsterdam** (p25) and New Year's Eve, and, of course, turning orange for the Netherlands' national holiday **King's Day** (Koningsdag; ⏱27 Apr), a celebration of the House of Orange, with hundreds of thousands of orange-clad locals and visitors filling Amsterdam's streets for drinking, dancing and buying and selling secondhand wares when the city becomes one big flea market.

De Pijp Shopping

inspired boutique every couple of weeks, keeping the selection up-to-the-minute. (www.bricklane-amsterdam.nl; Gerard Doustraat 80; ⏱1-6pm Mon, 10.30am-6pm Tue-Sat, 12.30-5.30pm Sun; Ⓜ De Pijp, 🚊24 Marie Heinekenplein)

Raak
FASHION & ACCESSORIES

24 🔒 MAP P124, B1

Unique casual clothing, bags, jewellery and homewares by Dutch and Scandinavian designers fill Raak's shelves and racks. (www.raakamsterdam.nl; 1e Van der Helststraat 46; ⏱10am-6pm Tue-Sat,

noon-6pm Sun & Mon; 🚊24 Marie Heinekenplein)

Tiller Galerie
ART

25 🔒 MAP P124, A1

This intimate, friendly gallery has works by George Heidweiller (check out the surreal Amsterdam skyscapes), Peter Donkersloot's portraits of animals and iconic actors such as Marlon Brando, and Herman Brood prints. (www.facebook.com/tillergalerie.amsterdam; 1e Jacob van Campenstraat 1; ⏱noon-6pm Wed-Sat; 🚊24 Marie Heinekenplein)

Explore
Oosterpark & East of the Amstel

Oost (East) is one of Amsterdam's most culturally diverse neighbourhoods. It grew up in the 19th century, with grand buildings and wide boulevards, and is now rapidly gentrifying, with hip bars, boutiques and restaurants popping up. The large English-style Oosterpark was laid out in 1861, while the lush Flevopark, further east, dates from when this area was a country retreat.

The Short List

○ **Tropenmuseum (p136)** Browsing the Museum of the Tropics' ethnographic collection.

○ **Dappermarkt (p140)** Sniffing out Turkish pide, kebabs and olives at Dappermarkt's food stalls.

○ **Oosterpark (p140)** Watching wild parakeets and heron in this peaceful park.

○ **De Kas (p141)** Dining in the greenhouse that grew the ingredients for your meal.

○ **Canvas (p143)** Clinking glasses to the sweeping city views from the city's coolest rooftop bar.

Getting There & Around

🚋 Tram 14 swings through the Oosterpark area on its east–west route. Tram 3 services the area via Museumplein.

🚌 No 757 from Centraal Station stops near Oosterpark.

Ⓜ The Wibautstraat stop is close to the Oost's south-west edge.

🚆 Muiderpoort station is handy for Javastraat.

Neighbourhood Map on p138

Parakeet, Oosterpark (p140) PHOTOGRAPHY BY ADRI/SHUTTERSTOCK ©

Top Experience
Examine Artefacts at Tropenmuseum

The gloriously quirky Tropenmuseum (Tropics Museum) has a whopping collection of ethnographic artefacts. Galleries surround a huge central hall across three floors and present exhibits with insight, imagination and lots of multimedia. The impressive arched building was built in 1926 to house the Royal Institute of the Tropics, and is still a leading research institute for tropical hygiene and agriculture.

◉ MAP P138, D2

📞 0880 042 800

www.tropenmuseum.nl

Linnaeusstraat 2

adult/child €16/8

🕙 10am-5pm Jul-Sep, closed Mon Oct-Jun

🚊 19 1e v.Swindenstraat

♿

Galleries

The Tropenmuseum's permanent collection, **Things That Matter**, addresses the social issues of what might happen to culture if a country disappears due to environmental issues.

There are also excellent **temporary exhibits**, which can range from the Hajj pilgrimage to Mecca and photographs of Aleppo to pop art and robots of Japan.

Tropenmuseum Junior

The museum has a kids' section, **Tropenmuseum Junior**, the first children's museum in the Netherlands, aimed at children from six to 13 years of age. It's great for hands-on fun, with loads of interactive exhibits.

Facilities

The museum's **gift shop** stocks enticing and unusual arts and crafts.

The on-site restaurant, **De Tropen** (☑020-568 20 00; www.amsterdamdetropen.nl; Linnaeusstraat 2; dishes €6.50-16; ☺10am-6pm; ⛾; ⛟19 1e v.Swindenstraat), has a lovely terrace and serves global cuisine, with a kids' menu available, too.

★ **Top Tips**

○ Get free admission to the museum and exhibitions with the I Amsterdam card (www.iamsterdam.com/en).

○ Buy your ticket online to avoid any queues.

✗ **Take a Break**

Duck across the road to Louie Louie (p141) for laid-back brasserie food in a convivial setting, with a glass-covered terrace for all weather.

Oosterpark & East of the Amstel Tropenmuseum

A B C D

1

Hoogte Kadijk

Nieuwe Keizersgracht
Nieuwe Keizersgr

14

Plantage Kerklaan

PLANTAGE Plantage Middenlaan

Artis Royal Zoo

7

NieuweKerkstr

Plantage Muidergr

Plantage Muidergracht

2

Nieuwe Prinsengracht
Nieuwe Prinsengr

Roetersstr

Sarphatistr

Alexanderkade

Nieuwe Achtergracht
Nieuwe Achtergr

Valckenierstr

7,19

Alexanderplein

Weesperstr

Weesper- plein

Valckenierstr

Sarphatistr

1,7,19

Spinozastr

's Gravesandestr

Mauritskade

Tropenmuseum 👁

Oosterpark
👁 **1**

3

M **Weesperplein**

Munten- damstr

Sajetplein

M Zeldenruststr

1

Oosterpark

Slavery Memorial

De Schreeuw ●

Mauritskade

Rhijnspoor- plein

1,3

Wibautstr

Ruyschstr

Onze Lieve Vrouwe Gasthuis

1,3

2e Oosterparkstr

4

Weesperzijde

11 👤

3

14 👤

✗ **9**

3e Oosterparkstr

1e Oosterparkstr

OOSTERPARKBUURT

Populierenweg

5

Amstel

Amsteldijk

Weesperzijde

G v Aemstelstr

M **Wibautstraat**

6

12 👤

Wibautstr

A B C D

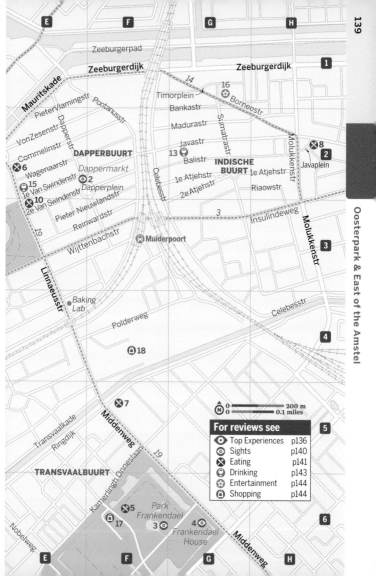

For reviews see

◉	Top Experiences	p136
◉	Sights	p140
✖	Eating	p141
🍷	Drinking	p143
★	Entertainment	p144
🛍	Shopping	p144

Sights

Oosterpark

PARK

1 ⊙ MAP P138, D3

The lush greenery of Oosterpark, with wild parakeets in the trees and herons stalking the large ponds, brings an almost tropical richness to this diverse neighbourhood, despite being laid out in English style. It was established in 1891 as a pleasure park for the diamond traders who found their fortunes in the South African mines, and it still has an elegant, rambling feel. (☉dawn-dusk; ♿; ☐19 1e v.Swindenstraat)

Dappermarkt

MARKET

2 ⊙ MAP P138, E2

The busy, untouristy Dappermarkt is a swirl of life and colour, with around 250 stalls. It reflects the Oost's diverse immigrant population, and is full of people (Africans, Turks, Dutch, hipsters), foods (apricots, olives, fish, Turkish kebabs) and goods from costume jewellery to cheap clothes, all sold from stalls lining the street. (www.dappermarkt.nl; Dapperstraat; ☉9am-5pm Mon-Sat; ☐1/3 Dapperstraat)

Park Frankendael

PARK

3 ⊙ MAP P138, F6

These lovely, landscaped gardens are the grounds of a former country estate; the mansion, Frankendael House, is still standing and there are walking paths, flapping storks, decorative bridges and the remains of follies. The excellent De Pure Markt (p145) is held here

De Kas

on the last Sunday of each month.
(www.huizefrankendael.nl; Middenweg;
 dawn-dusk; 🚊19 Hogeweg)

Frankendael House

HISTORIC BUILDING

4 MAP P138, G6

This area was rolling countryside several centuries ago. In the 18th century, wealthy Amsterdammers would pass their summers and weekends in large country retreats on a tract of drained land called Watergraafsmeer. There were once around 40 such mansions, but the last survivor is Frankendael, an elegant, restored Louis XIV–style mansion. Its formal gardens are open to the public daily. (www.huizefrankendael.nl; Middenweg 72; admission free; ⏱gardens dawn-dusk, house noon-5pm Sun; 🚊19 Hugo de Vrieslaan)

Eating

De Kas

INTERNATIONAL €€€

5 🍴 MAP P138, F6

In a row of stately greenhouses dating to 1926, De Kas has an organic attitude to match its chic glass setting. It grows most of its own herbs and produce right here and the result is incredibly pure flavours and innovative combinations. There's one set menu daily, based on whatever has been freshly harvested. Reserve in advance. (📞020-462 45 62; www.restaurantdekas.nl; Park Frankendael, Kamerlingh Onneslaan 3; 3-/4-course lunch menu €35/45, 5-/6-course

Ajax: Amsterdam's Football Team

High-tech complex **Johan Cruijff ArenA** (www.johancruijffarena.nl; Arena Blvd 1; 🛜; Ⓜ Bijlmer ArenA), with a retractable roof, is the home of four-times European champion Ajax, the Netherlands' most famous football team. Football games usually take place on Saturday evenings and Sunday afternoons from August to May. The arena also hosts big-name live-music shows. It's about 7km southeast of central Amsterdam, easily accessible by metro. Fans can also take a one-hour guided tour of the stadium (adult/child €16.50/11). See the website for the schedule.

dinner menu €57/65; ⏱noon-2pm & 6.30-10pm Mon-Fri, 6.30-10pm Sat; 🍴; 🚊19 Hogeweg)

Louie Louie

INTERNATIONAL €€

6 🍴 MAP P138, E2

With its rough wooden floorboards, big windows, fur-backed bar, model stags, squashy leather sofas and covered terrace, this relaxed brasserie-style place is perfect for a chilled-out meal. The menu is a fusion of Asian and Mexican dishes, from huevos rancheros in the morning to Asian salads, tacos, pork belly, burritos and wonton soup later in the day.

Vegan options, too. (☎020-370 29 81; www.louielouie.nl; Linnaeusstraat 11; dishes €7-15; ☺9am-1am Sun-Thu, to 3am Fri & Sat; ⚡; 🚊Muiderpoort)

Mr & Mrs Watson
VEGAN €€

7 🍴 MAP P138, F5

Named after the couple who coined the term 'veganism', this intimate, popular restaurant delivers wonderful plant-based comfort food. The seasonal menu might include sloppy joe chilli burgers of sliced seitan steak or vegan *bitterballen* 'better balls' with a Thai coconut curry filling. Don't miss the signature cheese platters and fondue – hard to believe it's not the real thing. (☎020-261 93 60; www.watsonsfood.com; Linnaeuskade 3h; lunch dishes €9-16, dinner mains €17-19; ☺11.30am-11.30pm; ⚡; 🚊19 Hogeweg)

Wilde Zwijnen
DUTCH €€

8 🍴 MAP P138, H2

The name means 'wild boar' and there's usually game on the menu in season at this modern Dutch restaurant. With pale walls and wood tables, the restaurant has a pared-down, rustic-industrial feel, and serves locally sourced, seasonal dishes with a creative twist. It's a meat-eater's paradise, but there's usually a vegetarian choice as well. (☎020-463 30 43; www.wildezwijnen.com; Javaplein 23; mains €20-27, 3-/4-course menus €34/40; ☺6-10pm Mon-Thu, noon-late Fri-Sun; 🛜; 🚊14 Javaplein)

Het IJsboefje
ICE CREAM €

9 🍴 MAP P138, C4

A popular ice-cream stop close to Oosterpark, with benches outside and tons of delicious flavours inside. There are always happy punters around, tucking into satisfyingly big portions of flavours such as *stroopwafel,* limoncello gelato and bright blue bubblegum Smurf – a winner with kids. (Beukenplein 5; 1/2/3 scoops €1.70/3.20/4; ☺noon-8pm, to 10pm Jun-Aug; 🚊3/7 Beukenweg)

Roopram Roti
SOUTH AMERICAN €

10 🍴 MAP P138, E3

This simple canteen-style Surinamese cafe often has a queue out the door, but it moves fairly fast. Place your order at the bar – the scrumptiously punchy and flaky lamb roti 'extra' (with egg) and the *barra* (lentil doughnut) are winners – and don't forget the fiery hot sauce. (1e Van Swindenstraat 4; mains €5.50-13.50; ☺2-9pm Tue-Sun; 🚊19 1e v.Swindenstraat)

Merkelbach
CAFE €€

The Merkelbach cafe (see 4 🔘 Map p138, G6) sits in the coach house adjoining Frankendael House (p141), and proffers dishes such as soups, salads and pastas with slow food credentials. Its patio is perfect for summer alfresco dining overlooking Frankendael's formal gardens, which are open to the public. (☎020-665 08 80; http://restaurantmerkelbach.nl; Mid-

denweg 72; dishes €7-14, lunch menu €32; ⏰8.30am-10.30pm Tue-Sat, to 6pm Sun & Mon; 🚊19 Hugo de Vrieslaan)

Drinking

De Ysbreeker

BROWN CAFE

11 🚇 MAP P138, A4

This gloriously historic but updated *bruin café* (traditional Dutch pub) first opened its doors in 1702. It's named after an icebreaker that used to dock in front to break the ice on the river during the winter months (stained-glass windows illustrate the scene). Inside, stylish drinkers hoist beverages in the plush booths and along the marble bar. (📞020-468 18 08; www.deysbreeker. nl; Weesperzijde 23; ⏰8am-1am Sun-Thu, to 2am Fri & Sat; 📶; 🚊3 Wibautstraat/Ruyschstraat)

Canvas

BAR

12 🚇 MAP P138, B5

Zoom up to the Volkshotel's 7th-floor bar for some of the best views in town, either through its large windows or on the open terrace. A creative-folk and hipster magnet, there are few better places for a drink in Amsterdam. On Sundays in winter, nonguests can head up to the rooftop for a dip in one of the hot tubs. (www. volkshotel.nl; Wibautstraat 150; ⏰7am-1am Mon-Thu, 7am-2am Fri, 8am-2am Sat, 8am-1am Sun; 📶; Ⓜ️Wibautstraat)

Baking Lab

Breathe in the scent of fresh baking in this open **bakery** (Map p138, E4; 📞020-240 01 58; www.bakinglab.nl; Linnaeusstraat 99; 3hr basic bread-making workshop €45, 1½hr kids workshop €20; ⏰8am-6pm Wed-Sat, to 5pm Sun; 🚊3/7 Linnaeusstraat), where workshops are offered for both adults and children. You can make your own bread here in the spirit of the old communal bakery, where people used to bring dough to knead and put in the shared oven, as few houses had ovens of their own.

You can also snack on hummus, sandwiches, vegan cakes or tarts (dishes €3.50 to €9.50).

Walter Woodbury Bar

BAR

13 🚇 MAP P138, G2

On rapidly gentrifying Javastraat, Walter Woodbury's Javanese-inspired, plant-filled and wooden interior has chesterfield lounges perfect for cosying into for expertly made classic cocktails and tasty bar snacks, including vegan *bitterballen* (deep-fried meatballs). Local beers on tap include Oedipus, Brouwerij 't IJ and Two Chefs, or sample one of the speciality G&Ts. (📞020-233 30 21; www.walterwoodburybar.nl; Javastraat 42; ⏰11am-1am Sun-Thu, to 3am Fri & Sat; 🚊Muiderpoort)

Roots Festival

Oosterpark plays host to a number of lively events during the summer and it's a great place to get a feel for the multicultural makeup of the neighbourhood. One highlight is the free global-music performances held on an open-air stage as part of the week-long Roots Festival (www.amsterdamroots.nl), which usually takes place in late June to early July at various venues around town.

4850

COFFEE

14 🔵 MAP P138, B4

From your morning caffeine fix to an evening tipple, hip cafe-bar 4850 has you covered. It turns out a great coffee along with an impressive selection of wines displayed across the rear wall. Natural light floods the industrial-meets-mid-century interior, while the outdoor pavement area is the ideal spot for sunny days. (www.4850.nl; Camperstraat 48-50; ⏲9am-11pm Mon, Tue & Thu, 9am-midnight Fri, 10am-midnight Sat, 10am-11pm Sun; 🛜; 🚊3 Camperstraat)

De Biertuin

BEER GARDEN

15 🔵 MAP P138, E2

With a covered terrace and heaters for chillier weather, 'the beer garden' attracts a young and beautiful crowd of locals with its lengthy beer list (around 16 on tap and over 50 more Dutch and Belgian varieties in bottles) and tasty pub food, such as burgers, burritos and fried chicken waffles. Mains €11 to €14. (🗗020-665 09 56; www.debiertuin.nl; Linnaeusstraat 29; ⏲11am-1am Sun-Thu, to 3am Fri & Sat; 🛜; 🚊19 1e v.Swindenstraat)

Entertainment

Studio K

ARTS CENTRE

16 ⭐ MAP P138, G1

This hip Oost arts centre always has something going on, with a cinema, a nightclub, a stage for bands and a theatre. There's also an eclectic restaurant, serving sandwiches and salads for lunch and vegetarian-friendly, international-flavoured dishes for dinner, and a huge terrace. (🗗020-692 04 22; www.studio-k.nu; Timorplein 62; ⏲11am-1am Sun-Thu, to 3am Fri & Sat; 🛜; 🚊14 Zeeburgerdijk)

Shopping

De Pure Markt

MARKET

17 🔒 MAP P138, F6

On the last Sunday of the month De Pure Markt sets up in Park Frankendael (p140), with artisanal and organic producers selling delicious gourmet foodstuffs. Peruse the market with a coffee or craft beer in hand, then grab a bite from the food stalls. Quality arts and crafts for sale include

Musician from band N3rdistan performing at Roots Festival

handwoven rugs, wooden chopping boards and fashion made from recycled materials. (www.puremarkt.nl; Park Frankendael; ⊙11am-6pm last Sun of month Mar-Dec; 🚊19 Hogeweg)

Het Faire Oosten

GIFTS & SOUVENIRS

18 🔒 MAP P138, F4

The perfect place to pick up an interesting gift or souvenir, Het Faire Oosten is stocked with beautiful homewares, quirky books, accessories and clothing by designers with an emphasis on sustainability. Check out the cool raincoats made from recycled plastic bottles, fair trade wooden kitchen utensils, vegan leather-look bags and eco-conscious yet still fashionable clothing made from organic cotton. (www.hetfaireoosten.nl; Waldenlaan 208; ⊙noon-6pm Mon, 10.30am-6pm Tue-Sat, noon-5pm Sun; 🚉Muiderpoort)

MELANIE LEMAHIEU/SHUTTERSTOCK ©

Explore

Nieuwmarkt, Plantage & the Eastern Islands

Buzzing Nieuwmarkt is sewn through with rich seams of history. Here you'll find Rembrandthuis – the master painter's studio – as well as insightful museums housed in centuries-old synagogues in the old Jewish quarter. Leafy Plantage is home to the sprawling zoo and botanical gardens, while the Eastern Islands has maritime history, ex-warehouses turned hip bars and flagship modern Dutch architecture.

The Short List

○ **Museum het Rembrandthuis (p148)** *Viewing Rembrandt's former home and studio.*

○ **Het Scheepvaartmuseum (p155)** *Fathoming the history of Dutch seafaring through this maritime collection.*

○ **Muziekgebouw aan 't IJ (p162)** *Catching live classical music or jazz at this stunning venue.*

○ **Verzetsmuseum (p155)** *Gaining an insight into the personal stories of the Dutch Resistance to the horrific WWII occupation.*

○ **Rederij Lampedusa (p161)** *Taking a fascinating tour on a former refugee boat.*

Getting There & Around

🚋 Tram 14 goes to Waterlooplein and the Jewish sights, as well as Plantage. Tram 7 goes to the Eastern Islands and Eastern Docklands. Tram 26 travels along the IJ River waterfront.

Ⓜ Lines 51, 53 and 54 stop at Waterlooplein and Nieuwmarkt.

Neighbourhood Map on p152

Het Scheepvaartmuseum (p155) DUTCHSCENERY/SHUTTERSTOCK ©

Top Experience 📷
Explore Museum het Rembrandthuis

Museum het Rembrandthuis provides an unparalleled insight into one of the Netherlands' greatest artistic geniuses, Rembrandt van Rijn. The museum occupies the three-storey canal house where the artist lived at the height of his success, and the interiors have been reconstructed according to a detailed inventory made when Rembrandt had to leave the house after his fortunes took a dive.

◎ MAP P152, B4

Rembrandt House Museum

☏ 020-520 04 00

www.rembrandthuis.nl

Jodenbreestraat 4

adult/child €14/5

🕙 10am-6pm

Ⓜ Waterlooplein

The House

The house dates from 1606. Rembrandt bought it for a fortune in 1639, made possible by his wealthy wife, Saskia van Uylenburgh. On the ground floor you'll see Rembrandt's living room–bedroom and the anteroom where he entertained clients.

Studio & Cabinet

Climb the narrow staircase and you'll come to the master's light-filled studio. Facing north and offering ideal light, this is where he painted masterpieces such as *The Night Watch*. The room is recognisable from an etching on display, and artists give demonstrations here on how Rembrandt sourced and mixed paints. Across the hall is Rembrandt's 'Cabinet', a room crammed with curiosities like those he collected: seashells, glassware, Roman busts and stuffed alligators.

Etchings

A small room is devoted to Rembrandt's famous etchings. The museum has a near-complete collection of them (about 250), although they're not all on display at once. Demonstrators crank up an oak press to show etching techniques several times daily.

Bankruptcy

The house was ultimately Rembrandt's financial undoing. As his work fell out of fashion, he was unable to pay off the mortgage, and in 1656 the house and its effects were sold to compensate his creditors. It's thanks to the debt collector's itemised list that the museum has been able to reproduce the interior so authentically. Rembrandt lived the rest of his years in cheaper digs in the Jordaan.

★ Top Tips

o I Amsterdam and Museumkaart cardholders get free entrance.

o It's worth checking out one of the many daily etching workshops.

o To avoid queues, book in advance online, or arrive early or late in the day.

o The free audioguide offers interesting details and insights.

✕ Take a Break

Have lunch at light-filled nearby cafe **TisFris** (www.tisfris. nl; St Antoniebreestraat 142; dishes €4.50-14; ◷9am-8pm; ᮀ14 Waterlooplein), only a few doors away.

Linger over a canal-side drink and snack at 17th-century charmer De Sluyswacht (p161), a charmingly wonky building right on the waterfront.

Walking Tour 🥾

Exploring Nieuwmarkt & Plantage

Thanks to Nieuwmarkt's action-packed plaza and the Plantage's garden-district greenery, the area makes for lively and lovely strolling. Distinctive cafes are the bonus here: they pop up in rustic shipping warehouses, 17th-century lock-keepers' quarters, the turreted city gate, and just about everywhere in between. A flea market and cool arts centre add to the daily buzz.

Walk Facts

Start Café Scharrebier

End Scheepvaarthuis

Length 3.5km; two hours

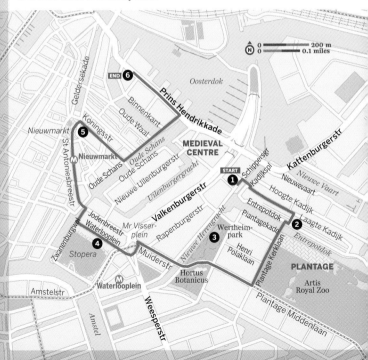

❶ Fuel up at Café Scharrebier

Join locals reading the newspaper and playing Scrabble at **Café Scharrebier** (📞020-624 81 01; www.scharrebier.nl; Rapenburgerplein 1; 🕐11am-1am Sun-Thu, to 3am Fri & Sat; 🚊22 Kadijksplein). Overlooking the lock, the terrace at this snug little *bruin café* (traditional Dutch pub) is an inviting spot for a beer, *jenever* (Dutch gin) or sandwich. *Scharrebier,* incidentally, was the name given to beer mixed with water to make it more affordable.

❷ Dockside at Entrepotdok

The Dutch East India Company, which grew rich on sea trade in the 17th century, owned **Entrepotdok** (🚊14 Plantage Kerklaan), a 500m row of warehouses that was the largest storage depot in Europe at the time. It's now packed with offices, apartments and dockside cafes perfect for lazing away a few hours at the water's edge, looking across to the Artis Royal Zoo.

❸ Wertheimpark's Memorial

Opposite the Hortus Botanicus, **Wertheimpark** (Plantage Parklaan; 🚊14 Artis) is a willow-shaded spot brilliant for lazing by the Nieuwe Herengracht – it's a great place to escape the crowds for a while. On the park's northeast side, locals often place flowers at the Auschwitz Memorial, a panel of broken mirrors installed in the ground that reflects the sky.

❹ Flea Market Finds

Covering the square once known as Vlooienburg (Flea Town), the **Waterlooplein Flea Market** (www.waterlooplein.amsterdam; Waterlooplein; 🕐9.30am-6pm Mon-Sat; Ⓜ Waterlooplein, 🚊14 Waterlooplein) draws sharp-eyed customers seeking everything from antique knick-knacks to designer knock-offs and cheap bicycle locks in amongst some tourist tat. The street market started in 1880, when Jewish traders living in the neighbourhood started selling their wares here.

❺ Fondue at Café Bern

Indulge in a dipping frenzy at the delightfully well-worn **Café Bern** (📞020-622 00 34; www.cafebern.com; Nieuwmarkt 9; mains €17-20; 🕐4pm-1am, kitchen 6-11pm; Ⓜ Nieuwmarkt). Locals have been coming here for more than 30 years for the Gruyère fondue and *entrecôte* (steak). Reservations advised.

❻ Scheepvaarthuis

Finish your walk with a nose around the supreme example of the Amsterdam School, **Scheepvaarthuis** (Shipping House; www.amrathamsterdam.com; Prins Hendrikkade 108; 🚊22/34/35 Prins Hendrikkade), with its nautical motifs, virtuoso stained glass and beautiful art-deco cafe. Now the Grand Hotel Amrath, staff are happy for tourists to look around.

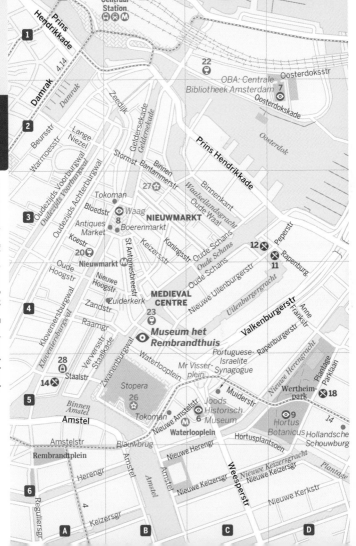

Centraal Station

Prins Hendrikkade

Damrak 4,14

1

2

Beursstr

Warmoesstr

Lange Niezel

Zeedijk

Oudezijds Voorburgwal

Oudezijds Achterburgwal

Gelderskade

Stormst

Binnen Bantammerstr

22

OBA: Centrale Bibliotheek Amsterdam **7**

Oosterdokstr

Oosterdokskade

Oosterdok

Prins Hendrikkade

Binnenkant

Waalseilandsgracht

Oude Waal

Tokoman

Bloedstr

Antiques Market

8 Waag

NIEUWMARKT

Boerenmarkt

27

3

Koestr

20

Nieuwmarkt

St Antoniesbreestr

Keizersstr

Koningsstr

Oude Schans

Oude Schans

12

Peperstr

11

Rapenburg

Oude Hoogstr

Nieuwe Hoogstr

Zandstr

Raamgr

Zuiderkerk

23

MEDIEVAL CENTRE

Nieuwe Uilenburgerstr

Uilenburgergracht

Valkenburgerstr

Anne Frankstr

4

Kloveniersburgwal

Verversstr

Staalkade

Museum het Rembrandthuis

Zwanenburgwal

Waterlooplein

Mr Visserplein

Portugese-Israelite Synagogue

Rapenburgerstr

Nieuwe Herengracht

Plantage

Parklaan

28

14

Staalstr

Stopera

26

Tokoman

Binnen Amstel

Amstel

Nieuwe Amstelstr

Waterlooplein

Muiderstr

Joods Historisch Museum **6**

Hortusplantsoen

Wertheimpark

18

Hortus Botanicus **9**

Hollandsche Schouwburg

14

Amstelstr

Rembrandtplein

Herengr

Blauwbrug

Amstel

Nieuwe Herengr

Nieuwe Kelzersgr

Nieuwe Kelzersgr

Weesperstr

Nieuwe Kerkstr

6

Reguliersgr

Keizersgr

4

E
☆ 25

F

G

Javabrug
⊗ 🔒
16 29

H

1

Jollemanhof

Piet Heinkade

26

For reviews see

⊙ Top Experiences p148
◉ Sights p154
⊗ Eating p158
🍺 Drinking p160
☆ Entertainment p162
🛍 Shopping p163

🍺 21

Dijksgracht

Ⓝ 0 _____ 200 m
0 _____ 0.1 miles

2

IJ Tunnel

NEMO
5 ◉ Science
Museum

Kattenburg

OOSTELIJKE
EILANDEN

Wittenburg

3

Historic
Barges

Het Scheepvaartmuseum ◉ 3

Kattenburgerstr

Grote Wittenburgerstr
Kleine Wittenburgerstr

10 ◉ ARCAM

Kattenburgerplein

Wittenburgergr

Oostenburgervoorstr

4

Kadijkspl
⊗ 19

Nieuwevaart

Overhaalsgang

13 ⊗ Oostenburgergr

Czaar
Peterstr

Laagte Kadijk

Nieuwe Vaart

Plantagekade

Entrepotdok
Entrepotdok

Hoogte Kadijk

Oostenburgergr

5

Verzetsmuseum
4 ◉

PLANTAGE

24 🍺

Plantage
kerklaan

◉ 1 Artis Royal Zoo
◉ 2 Micropia
⊗ 17

Sarphatistr

Alexanderkade

⊗
15

Plantage Middenlaan

Artis Royal
Zoo

Mauritskade

6

Plantage Muidergr

Muidergracht

Artis Aquarium &
Artis Zoological
Museum

E

F

G

H

Sights

Artis Royal Zoo

ZOO

1  MAP P152, E5

A wonderfully leafy expanse, mainland Europe's oldest zoo has a fine range of wildlife, with extensive habitats and room to wander. A lovely stretch runs along the canal looking across to the old Entrepot (p151) dock. Habitats include African savannah and tropical rainforest, and there are reptiles, lions, jaguars, elephants, giraffes and lots of primates. There's also an aquarium complex featuring coral reefs, shark tanks and an Amsterdam canal displayed from a fish's point of view, plus a planetarium and kids petting zoo. (📞020-523 34 00; www.artis.nl; Plantage Kerklaan

38-40; adult/child €24/20.50, incl Micropia €30.50/26.50; 🕙9am-6pm Mar-Oct, to 5pm Nov-Feb; 🚊14 Artis)

Micropia

MUSEUM

2  MAP P152, E5

The world's first microbe museum is a germaphobe's nightmare. Micropia has hands-on exhibits and microscopes to peer through and fascinating, if unsettling, facts about how many living organisms there are around us everyday. Dare to take a body scan and become acquainted with your own microorganisms and learn the unromantic side of locking lips via the kiss-o-meter. There are also glass models of viruses from ebola to smallpox. It's aimed at those aged eight and over. (📞020-523 36 71; www.

View of Zuiderkerk down Groenburgwal

DENNISVDW/GETTY IMAGES ©

micropia.nl; Artisplein, Plantage Kerklaan 38-40; adult/child €15/13, incl Artis Royal Zoo €30.50/26.50; ⏰9am-6pm Sun-Wed, to 8pm Thu-Sat; 🚊14 Artis)

Het Scheepvaartmuseum   MUSEUM

3 ◉ MAP P152, E3

A waterfront 17th-century admiralty building houses this state-of-the-art presentation of maritime memorabilia. Highlights include imaginatively presented Golden Age maps, fascinating 19th-century photos of early voyages and an audiovisual, immersive journey evoking a voyage by ship. There's plenty to keep the kids interested, too. Outside, you can clamber over the full-scale replica of the 700-tonne *Amsterdam* – one of the largest ships in the Dutch East India Company fleet – with its tiny bunks and sailors' hammocks, and admire the **Royal Barge** in the boathouse. (Maritime Museum; 📞020-523 22 22; www.hetscheepvaartmuseum. nl; Kattenburgerplein 1; adult/child €16.50/8; ⏰9am-5pm; 🚊22/48 Kattenburgerplein)

Verzetsmuseum   MUSEUM

4 ◉ MAP P152, E5

The museum of the Dutch Resistance brings the horror of German occupation in WWII vividly alive, using personal stories, letters, artefacts, films and photographs to illuminate local resistance to (but also collaboration with) the

Groenburgwal and the Zuiderkerk

Step out onto the white Staalmeestersbrug drawbridge that crosses the Groenburgwal and look north towards the **Zuiderkerk** (Map p152, B4; 📞020-308 03 99, tower tours 020-689 25 65; www.zuiderkerkamsterdam. nl; Zuiderkerkhof 72; Ⓜ Nieuwmarkt) for one of Amsterdam's prettiest canal views. Impressionist Claude Monet certainly took a shining to it, and painted it in 1874 as *The Zuiderkerk (South Church) at Amsterdam: Looking up the Groenburgwal*.

Nazis. There's also a section on the Dutch East Indies (now Indonesia) pre- and postwar. Labels are in Dutch and English, and there is a free audioguide available in multiple languages. Allow at least a couple of hours to explore the museum. (Dutch Resistance Museum; 📞020-620 25 35; www. verzetsmuseum.org; Plantage Kerklaan 61; adult/child €11/6; ⏰10am-5pm Mon-Fri, 11am-5pm Sat & Sun; 🚊14 Plantage Kerklaan)

NEMO Science Museum   SCIENCE CENTRE

5 ◉ MAP P152, E2

Perched atop the entrance to the IJ Tunnel is this unmissable green-copper building with a slanted roof, designed by Italian

The Dutch Golden Age

The Golden Age spans roughly the 17th century, when Holland was at the peak of its powers. It's the era when Rembrandt painted, when city planners built the canals and when Dutch ships conquered the seas.

It started when trading rival Antwerp was retaken by the Spaniards in the late 16th century, and merchants, skippers and artisans flocked to Amsterdam. A new moneyed society emerged. Persecuted Jews from Portugal and Spain also fled to Amsterdam. Not only did they introduce the diamond industry, they also knew of trade routes to the West and East Indies.

Enter the Dutch East India Company, which wrested the Asian spice trade from the Portuguese. It soon grew into the world's richest corporation, with more than 50,000 employees and a private army. Its sister, the Dutch West India Company, traded with Africa and the Americas and was at the centre of the American slave trade. In 1672 Louis XIV of France invaded the Low Countries, and the era known as the Dutch Golden Age ended.

architect Renzo Piano and almost surrounded by water. Its rooftop square has great views and water- and wind-operated hands-on exhibits. Inside, everything is interactive, with four floors of investigative mayhem kids of all ages will enjoy. Experiment with lifting yourself up via a pulley, making bubbles, building structures, dividing light into colours, racing your shadow, watching a chain-reaction display and discovering the teenage mind. (☏020-244 01 81; www.nemosciencemuseum.nl; Oosterdok 2; €17.50, roof terrace free; ⏰10am-5.30pm, closed Mon early Sep-early Feb, roof terrace to 9pm Jul & Aug; 👪; 🚊22/48 Kadijksplein)

Joods Historisch Museum

MUSEUM

6 ◉ MAP P152, C5

In this beautifully restored complex of four Ashkenazic synagogues from the 17th and 18th centuries, displays show the history of Jews in the Netherlands, including the rise of Jewish enterprise and its role in the Dutch economy. An excellent audioguide is included and there's a small children's museum with some activities. Tickets also include admission to all of the Joods Cultureel Kwartier (Jewish Cultural Quarter) sites, including the **Portuguese-Israelite Synagogue** (www.jck.nl; Mr Visserplein 3; adult/child 13-17yr/child 6-12yr/under 6yr €17/8.50/4.25/free; ⏰10am-5pm

Sun-Fri May-Aug, 10am-5pm Sun-Thu, to 4pm Fri Mar, Apr, Sep & Oct, reduced hours Nov-Feb; M Waterlooplein) and the **Hollandsche Schouwburg** (National Holocaust Museum, Holland Theatre; ☎ 020-531 03 10; www.jck.nl; Plantage Middenlaan 24; adult/child 13-17yr/child 6-12yr/under 6yr €17/8.50/4.25/free; ◷ 11am-5pm; ፼ 14 Artis). (Jewish Historical Museum; ☎ 020-531 03 10; www.jck.nl; Nieuwe Amstelstraat 1; adult/child 13-17yr/child 6-12yr/under 6yr €17/8.50/4.25/free; ◷ 11am-5pm; M Waterlooplein)

OBA: Centrale Bibliotheek Amsterdam

LIBRARY

7 ◉ MAP P152, D2

This being Amsterdam, it has one of the coolest libraries you can imagine, built in 2007 and spread over multiple light, bright floors. The basement is devoted to kids, and has a wigwam, a huge polar bear and the magical, marvellous Mouse Mansion, with 100 beautifully detailed rooms, the work of artist Karina Content. On the 7th floor is the reasonably priced food court, where an outdoor terrace offers thrilling panoramic views across the water to Amsterdam's old town. (Amsterdam Central Library; ☎ 020-523 09 00; www.oba.nl; Oosterdokskade 143; admission free; ◷ 8am-10pm Mon-Fri, 10am-10pm Sat & Sun; ⌖; ፼ 4/12/14/24/26 Centraal Station)

Waag

HISTORIC BUILDING

8 ◉ MAP P152, B3

The multi-turreted Waag was built as a gate in the city walls in 1488.

In 1601 the walls were destroyed to allow the city to expand, and the building was turned into Amsterdam's main weigh house, and later a spot for public executions. A bar-restaurant occupies it today. Out the front, Nieuwmarkt hosts a variety of events, including a Saturday farmers market and a Sunday antiques market. (www.indewaag.nl; Nieuwmarkt 4; ◷ bar-restaurant 11am-11pm Mon-Wed, from 9am Thu-Sat; M Nieuwmarkt)

Hortus Botanicus

GARDENS

9 ◉ MAP P152, D5

A botanical garden since 1638, it bloomed as tropical seeds and plants were brought in by Dutch trading ships. From here, coffee, pineapple, cinnamon and palm-oil plants were distributed throughout the world. The 4000-plus species are kept in wonderful structures, including the colonial-era seed house and a three-climate glasshouse. (Botanical Garden; ☎ 020-625 90 21; www.dehortus.nl; Plantage Middenlaan 2a; adult/child/under 5yr €9.75/5.50/free; ◷ 10am-5pm; ፼ 14 Mr Visserplein)

ARCAM

ARCHITECTURE

10 ◉ MAP P152, E3

The curved Amsterdam Architecture Foundation, a striking waterside building designed by Dutch architect René van Zuuk, hosts changing architectural exhibitions plus Architecture Talk & Walk tours (€24.50). The tours consist of a 45-minute lecture followed by a

MARTIN MOOS/LONELY PLANET ©

Hortus Botanicus (p157)

guided two-hour walk, and run on Fridays at 1.30pm from April to October. (Stichting Architectuur-centrum Amsterdam; ☎020-620 48 78; www.arcam.nl; Prins Hendrikkade 600; admission free; ⏰1-5pm Tue-Sun; 🚊22/48 Kadijksplein)

Eating

Greetje
DUTCH €€€

11 ✖ MAP P152, D3

Greetje is Amsterdam's most creative Dutch restaurant, using the best seasonal produce to resurrect and re-create traditional recipes, such as slow-cooked veal with Dutch-brandy-marinated apricots and suckling pork in apple syrup with Dutch mustard sauce. The tasting menu (€55) starts with the Big Beginning, a selection of six starters served high-tea style. (☎020-779 74 50; www.restaurantgreetje.nl; Peperstraat 23-25; mains €24-29; ⏰6-10pm; 🚊22/48 Prins Hendrikkade)

Gebr Hartering
DUTCH €€€

12 ✖ MAP P152, C3

Lined in pale rustic wood, this gem was founded by two food-loving brothers, who offer either à la carte or a multi-course menu that changes daily according to the best seasonal produce available. A meal here is always a delight to linger over, so settle in and enjoy the accompanying wines and peaceful canal-side location. (☎020-421 06 99; www.gebr-hartering.nl; Peperstraat 10; mains €27.50, 5-/7-course menus €55/80; ⏰6-10.30pm; 🚊22/48 Prins Hendrikkade)

Frank's Smokehouse

SEAFOOD €€

13 MAP P152, G4

Frank is a prime supplier to Amsterdam's restaurants, and you can try his renowned smoked fish and meats at this smart deli-restaurant. Delicious takeaway sandwiches (smoked halibut, truffle cheese or warm smoked ham with relish) are available from the deli, or dine in on smoked fish platters, king crab or smoked brisket, along with their excellent beer featuring smoked malt. (☎020-585 71 07; www.smokehouse.nl; Oostenburgervoorstraat 1; platters from €16, mains €15-24, sandwiches from €3.50; ⊙deli 10am-7pm Tue-Fri, 9am-6pm Sat, 10am-6pm Sun, restaurant 11.30am-10pm Tue-Sat, to 6pm Sun; ☐22 Wittenburgergracht)

Sterk Staaltje

DELI €

14 MAP P152, A5

With pristine fruit and veg stacked up outside, Sterk Staaltje is worth entering just to breathe in the scent of the foodstuffs, with a fine range of ready-to-eat treats: teriyaki meatballs, spinach and pumpkin quiche, filling salads and hearty soups. The sandwiches are particularly fantastic – roast beef, horseradish and rucola (arugula/rocket) or marinated chicken with guacamole and sour cream. (www.sterkstaaltje.com; Staalstraat 12; dishes €4-10; ⊙8.30am-7pm Mon-Fri, 8.30am-6pm Sat, 10am-7pm Sun; ☐24 Muntplein)

Tokoman: Surinamese Spice

Queue with the folks getting their Surinamese spice on at **Tokoman** (Map p152, B5; www.tokoman.nl; Waterlooplein 327; sandwiches €3.75-5.50, dishes €6.50-12.50; ⊙11am-7pm Mon-Sat; Ⓜ Waterlooplein). It makes a sensational *broodje pom,* a sandwich filled with a tasty mash of chicken and a starchy Surinamese tuber. You'll want the *zuur* (pickled-cabbage relish) and *peper* (chilli) on it, plus a cold can of coconut water to wash it down.

There's another **branch** (Map p152, B3; www.tokoman.nl; Zeedijk 136; sandwiches €3.75-5.50, dishes €6.50-12.50; ⊙11.30am-9.30pm; Ⓜ Nieuwmarkt) close by.

Box Sociaal

INTERNATIONAL €€

15 MAP P152, E5

Set up by two Aussies, this stylish neighbourhood cafe opposite the zoo (p154) has you covered any time of the day. Brunch on smashed avo on toast, enjoy all-day pub grub, including an Aussie-style chicken parma, or settle in for a more upmarket dinner of caramelised four-hour-braised beef cheek with Asian slaw, paired with a *stroopwafel* espresso martini. (☎020-280 55 78; www.boxsociaal.com; Plantage Middenlaan 30a; dishes €8-23; ⊙9am-11pm; ☎; ☐14 Artis)

Bonboon

VEGAN €€

16 MAP P152, G1

A sign on the wall reads 'eat beans, not beings' at this creative vegan restaurant opposite the water, with so much more than beans on the menu. Start with beluga lentil and cauliflower cream with truffle oil, then move on to mains such as portobello pie. Dishes are superbly presented and there's a great terrace next to bobbing houseboats. (📞 06 1809 8855; www.bonboon.nl; Piraeusplein 59; mains €19, 3-course menu €35; ⏰ 6-10pm Wed & Thu, from 1-10pm Fri-Sun; 🍴; 🚋 7 Azartplein)

De Plantage

EUROPEAN €€

17 MAP P152, E5

Huge and graceful, this is an impressive space in an 1870s-built, 1900-expanded former greenhouse decked with blond wood and black chairs, and offering views of the Artis Royal Zoo (p154) aviary. Food is creative and tasty, including ravioli filled with wild boar ragu, and Iberian pork belly with carrot cream and roasted celeriac. Unfortunately the service can be a letdown. (📞 020-760 68 00; www.caferestaurant deplantage.nl; Plantage Kerklaan 36; lunch mains €7.50-21.50, dinner mains €19.50-23.50; ⏰ kitchen 9am-10pm Mon-Fri, 10am-10pm Sat & Sun, bar to 1am; 🚋 14 Plantage Kerklaan)

Café Smit en Voogt

CAFE €€

18 MAP P152, D5

On a leafy corner, with high ceilings and a relaxed vibe, this cool and laid-back cafe is ideal for a salad or sandwich for lunch, or a coffee and slice of apple pie when visiting Museum het Rembrandt Huis (p148) or the adjacent Wertheimpark (p151). There's also a more substantial dinner menu. (http://cafesmitenvoogt.nl; Plantage Parklaan 10; lunch mains €6-10, dinner mains €14-20; ⏰ kitchen 10am-9.30pm, bar to 1am; 📶; 🚋 14 Plantage Kerklaan)

Café Kadijk

INDONESIAN €€

19 MAP P152, E4

This snug split-level cafe with leaf-print wallpaper is popular for its excellent, good-value Indonesian food, including a mini €20 version of the normally gigantic rijsttafel (Indonesian banquet). There's a big terrace with views across the water in summer. No credit cards. (📞 06 1774 4441; www.cafekadijk.nl; Kadijksplein 5; mains €15-20; ⏰ 4pm-1am Sun-Thu, to 3am Fri & Sat, kitchen 4-10pm; 🚋 22/48 Kadijksplein)

Drinking

Rosalia's Menagerie

COCKTAIL BAR

20 MAP P152, A3

Named after the owner's grandmother, this charming bar in the canal-side boutique hotel Misc EatDrinkSleep feels like your grandma's living room with its rich floral wallpaper, knick-knacks and baroque armchairs. It serves expertly made tipples focusing on Dutch heritage, including

jenever-based cocktails and organic wines, and a small menu of tasty snacks. Best to book a table ahead on weekends. (☏020-330 62 41; www.rosalias.amsterdam; Kloveniersburgwal 20; ⊙6pm-late; Ⓜ Nieuwmarkt)

Hannekes Boom
BEER GARDEN

21 MAP P152, E1

Reachable via a couple of pedestrian/bike bridges from the NEMO Science Museum (p155), this cool, laid-back waterside *café* is built from recycled materials and has a fantastic leafy beer garden. Join the arty crowd enjoying the sunshine at brightly coloured picnic tables under the trees. If the weather's no good, cosy into a vintage armchair by the fire inside. (☏020-419 98 20; www.hannekes boom.nl; Dijksgracht 4; ⊙11am-1am Sun-Thu, to 3am Fri & Sat; ⓐ26 Muziekgebouw)

SkyLounge
COCKTAIL BAR

22 MAP P152, C1

With wow-factor views whatever the weather, this bar offers a 360-degree panorama of Amsterdam from the 11th floor of the DoubleTree Amsterdam Centraal Station hotel – and it gets better when you head out to its vast SkyTerrace, with an outdoor bar. Toast the view with a huge range of cocktails, craft beers and spirits. DJs regularly hit the decks from 9pm. (☏020-530 08 75; www. skyloungeamsterdam.com; Oosterdoksstraat 4; ⊙11am-1am Sun-Tue, to

Rederij Lampedusa

Take a two-hour canal-boat tour around Amsterdam harbour in former refugee **boats** (http://rederijlampedusa.nl/en; 2hr canal tour €19; ⊙canal tours 11am & 1.30pm Sat May-Sep), brought from Lampedusa (Italy) by Dutch founder Tuen. The tours are full of heart and offer a fascinating insight, not only into stories of contemporary migration, but also about how immigration shaped Amsterdam's history – especially the canal tour. Departs from next to Mediamatic.

2am Wed & Thu, to 3am Fri & Sat; 🛜; ⓐ4/12/14/24/26 Centraal Station)

De Sluyswacht
BROWN CAFE

23 MAP P152, B4

Out on a limb by the canal and listing like a ship in high winds, this tiny black building dating to 1695 was once a lock-keeper's house on the Oude Schans. The canal-side terrace with views of the Montelbaanstoren is a charming spot to relax with a Dutch or Belgian beer and bar snacks, including *bitterballen* (deep-fried meatballs), chips and toasties. (☏020-625 76 11; www.sluyswacht. nl; Jodenbreestraat 1; ⊙12.30pm-1am Mon-Thu, to 3am Fri & Sat, to 7pm Sun; Ⓜ Waterlooplein; ⓐ14 Waterlooplein)

Local Markets

In addition to the sprawling **Waterlooplein Flea Market** (p151), other markets in this area include the **Antiques Market** (Map p152, B3; Nieuwmarkt; ⏰9am-5pm Sun; Ⓜ Nieuwmarkt) and **Boerenmarkt** (Farmers Market; Map p152, B3; Nieuwmarkt; ⏰9am-4pm Sat; Ⓜ Nieuwmarkt), which both take place on Nieuwmarkt.

Brouwerij 't IJ
BREWERY

24 ✪ MAP P152, H5

Can you get more Dutch than drinking a craft beer beneath the creaking sails of the 1725-built De Gooyer Windmill? Amsterdam's leading microbrewery makes delicious standard, seasonal and limited-edition brews; try the smooth, fruity 'tripel' Zatte, which was their first creation back in 1985. Enjoy yours in the tiled tasting room, lined by an amazing bottle collection, or the plane-tree-shaded terrace. (www.brouwerijhetij.nl; Funenkade 7; ⏰brewery 2-8pm, English tour 3.30pm Fri-Sun; 🚊7 Hoogte Kadijk)

Entertainment

Muziekgebouw aan 't IJ
CONCERT VENUE

25 ✪ MAP P152, E1

A dramatic glass-and-steel box on the IJ waterfront, this multidisciplinary performing-arts venue has a state-of-the-art main hall with flexible stage layout and great acoustics. Its jazz stage, **Bimhuis** (☎020-788 21 88; www.bimhuis.nl; Piet Heinkade 3; 🚊26 Muziekgebouw), is more intimate. Try the Last Minute Ticket Shop (www.lastminuteticketshop.nl) for discounts. (☎tickets 020-788 20 00; www.muziekgebouw.nl; Piet Heinkade 1; ⏰box office 2-6pm Mon-Sat; 🚊26 Muziekgebouw)

Muziektheater
CLASSICAL MUSIC

26 ✪ MAP P152, B5

The Muziektheater is home to the Netherlands Opera and the National Ballet, with some spectacular performances. Big-name performers and international dance troupes also take the stage here. Free classical concerts (12.30pm to 1pm) are held most Tuesdays from September to June in its Boekmanzaal; doors open at 12.15pm. (☎020-625 54 55; www.operaballet.nl; Waterlooplein 22; ⏰box office noon-6pm Mon-Fri, to 3pm Sat & Sun or until performance Sep-Jul; Ⓜ Waterlooplein, 🚊14 Waterlooplein)

Amsterdams Marionetten Theater
PUPPETRY

27 ✪ MAP P152, B3

An enchanting enterprise that seems to exist in another era, this marionette theatre presents fairy tales and Mozart operas, such as *The Magic Flute*, in a former blacksmith's shop. Kids and adults

Waterlooplein Flea Market (p151)

alike are enthralled by the magical stage sets, period costumes and beautiful singing voices that bring the diminutive cast to life. (☎020-620 80 27; www.marionettentheater.nl; Nieuwe Jonkerstraat 8; adult/child €16/7.50, 90-min tour €15; Ⓜ Nieuwmarkt)

Shopping

Hôtel Droog
DESIGN

28 🔒 MAP P152, A5

Not a hotel, but a local design house. Droog means 'dry' in Dutch, and these products are full of dry wit. You'll find all kinds of stylish versions of useful things – a clothes-hanger lamp or streamlined hot water bottle – as well as the kind of clothing that should probably by law only be worn by a designer or an architect. (www.droog.com; Staalstraat 7; ⏰9am-7pm; 🚊24 Muntplein)

Pols Potten
HOMEWARES

29 🔒 MAP P152, H1

The Eastern Islands are particularly style conscious, and the go-to shop for local residents, as well as stylish Amsterdammers from all over, is this large interior-design store. With plenty of hip colourful furniture, as well as fabulous ceramics and hand-blown glassware, it's a good spot to pick up a gift or souvenir. (☎020-419 35 41; www.polspotten.nl; Loods 6, KNSM-laan 39; ⏰10am-6pm Tue-Sat, noon-5pm Sun; 🚊7 Azartplein)

Explore ⬡

Amsterdam Noord

Amsterdam Noord, a quick free ferry ride across the IJ River from central Amsterdam, is a previously neglected area that has been reinvented as the city's hippest neighbourhood. It encompasses ex-industrial areas, cutting-edge architecture, and hangars turned hipster hangouts with walls covered in street art, all minutes away from fields, horses and the odd windmill.

The Short List

○ **A'DAM Tower (p167)** *Taking in the view from this skyscraper.*

○ **Nieuwendammerdijk (p167)** *Meandering along this enchantingly pretty narrow dyke of wooden houses, surrounded by flowers, greenery and birdsong.*

○ **EYE Film Institute (p168)** *Admiring the angular, gleaming white architecture of the IJ-side Eye, with its cinema-focused exhibitions.*

○ **Kunststad (p167)** *Exploring the artist studios in this massive former warehouse, with artworks dangling from the ceiling and enough room to cycle around.*

○ **Bars, cafes & restaurants (p169)** *Hanging out at one of Noord's ultra-cool bar-cafe-restaurants, such as Pllek.*

Getting There & Around

⛴ There are free 24-hour ferries between Amsterdam Centraal Station, Buiksloterweg, NDSM and IJplein.

Ⓜ The North-South line 52 links Amsterdam Zuid in the south with Noorderpark and Noord stations via Amsterdam Centraal Station.

Neighbourhood Map on p166

A'DAM Tower (p167) ITZAVU/SHUTTERSTOCK © ARCHITECT: ARTHUR STAAL

Amsterdam Noord

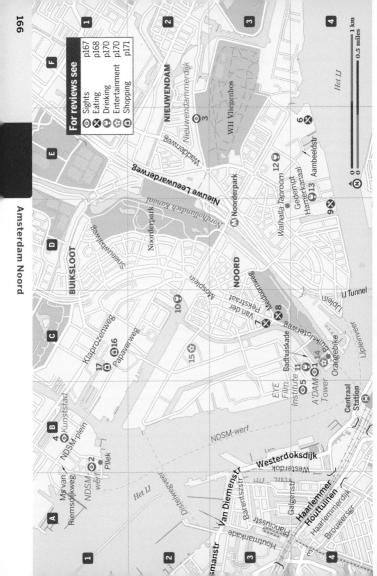

For reviews see

☉	Sights	p167
✕	Eating	p168
◐	Drinking	p170
✿	Entertainment	p170
🛍	Shopping	p171

NIEUWENDAM

Nieuwendammerdijk

Waddenweg

WH Vliegenbos

Nieuwe Leeuwarderweg

Noordhollandsch kanaal

Noorderpark

BUIKSLOOT

Sneeuwbalweg

Noorderpark

Mosplein

M Noorderpark

NOORD

Meeuwenlaan

Klaprozenweg

Papaverweg

Van der Pekstraat

Buiksloterweg

IJplein

IJ Tunnel

Walhalla Taproom

Gedempt Hamerkanaal

Aambeeldstr

Het IJ

EYE Film Institute

Badhuiskade

A'DAM Tower

Orangebike

Centraal Station

IJpleinveer

NDSM-werf

Westerdoksdijk

Westerdok

Het IJ

Distelweg

Ms van Riemsdijkweg

NDSM-plein

Kunststad

NDSM-werf

Pliek

Distelweg

Van Diemenstr

Houttuinen

Haarlemmer Houttuinen

Haarlemmerdijk

Brouwersgr

Houthenstr

Barentszstr

Planciusstr

Galgenstr

Houtmankade

Haarlemmerplein

1 km
0.5 miles

Sights

A'DAM Tower

NOTABLE BUILDING

1 MAP P166, C4

The 22-storey A'DAM Tower used to be the Royal Dutch Shell oil company offices, but has had a makeover to become one of Amsterdam's biggest attractions. Take the trippy lift to the rooftop for awe-inspiring views in all directions, with a giant six-person swing that kicks out over the edge (you're well secured and strapped in) for those who have a head for heights. (www.adamlookout.com; Overhoeksplein 1; lookout adult/child/family €13.50/7.50/32, swing €5; ⏱ lookout 10am-10pm, last admission 9pm; 🚢 Buiksloterweg)

NDSM-werf

AREA

2 MAP P166, B1

This derelict shipyard turned edgy arts community, 15 minutes upriver from the city centre, wafts a post-apocalyptic vibe. Abandoned trams rust by the water's edge, and street art is splashed on most surfaces. Young creatives hang out at the smattering of cool cafes, and hip businesses such as MTV and Red Bull have their European headquarters here. The area is also a centre for the **Over het IJ Festival** (www.overhetij. nl; ⏱ mid-Jul; 🚢 NDSM-werf), and other underground culture and events. (www.ndsm.nl; NDSM-plein; 🚢 NDSM-werf)

Cycling in Amsterdam Noord

The best way to explore Noord is via bike. Places are spread out, there isn't much traffic and there are lots of cycle routes. You can take bikes on the free ferries, or hire one on the Noord side through **Orangebike** (Map p166, C4; 📞 06 4684 2083; www. orange-bike.nl; Buiksloterweg 5c; tours €22.50-37.50, hire per hour/day from €5/11; ⏱ 9am-6pm; 🚢 Buiksloterweg).

Nieuwendammerdijk

STREET

3 MAP P166, E2

Enchanting chocolate-box prettiness characterises this long, narrow street of wooden Dutch houses, now prime real estate, with hollyhocks nodding beside every porch. Many houses date from the 1500s, and numbers 202 to 204 were where the shipbuilding family De Vries Lentsch lived. Numbers 301 to 309 were once captains' houses. (🚌 32 Buikslotermeerplein)

Kunststad

ART STUDIO

4 MAP P166, B1

This former shipbuilding warehouse is filled with over 80 artists studios, with some 250 artists working in the NDSM *broedplaats* (breeding ground). It's a big enough space that you can cycle or walk around the area, with huge

artworks hanging from the ceiling, and structures within the hangar. There is a visitor centre for information and to buy artworks, and the exhibition space NDSM Fuse – both are open noon to 6pm Friday to Sunday. (Art City NDSM; www.ndsmloods.nl; NDSM-plein; admission free; ⏰8am-6pm; 🚊NDSM-werf)

EYE Film Institute

MUSEUM, CINEMA

5 🔘 MAP P166, B4

At this modernist architectural triumph that seems to balance on its edge on the banks of the IJ (also pronounced 'eye') River, the institute screens movies from its 40,000-title archive in four theatres, sometimes with live music. Exhibitions of costumes, digital art and other cinephile amusements run in conjunction with what's playing. A view-tastic bar-restaurant with a fabulously sunny terrace (when the sun makes an appearance) is a popular hangout on this side of the river. (📞020-589 14 00; www.eyefilm.nl; IJpromenade 1; adult/child exhibitions €11/free, films €11/7.50; ⏰exhibitions 10am-7pm; 🚊Buiksloterweg)

Eating

Hotel de Goudfazant

FRENCH €€

6 🍴 MAP P166, E4

With a name taken from lyrics of the Jacques Brel song 'Les Bourgeois', this extraordinary gourmet hipster restaurant spreads through a cavernous former garage, still

EYE Film Institute

raw and industrial, and sticks to the theme by having cars parked inside. Rockstar-looking chefs cook up a French-influenced storm in the open kitchen. There is no hotel, FYI, except in name. (📞020-636 51 70; www.hoteldegoudfazant.nl; Aambeeldstraat 10h; 3-course menu €32; ⏱6pm-midnight Tue-Sun; 🚊IJplein, Ⓜ️Noorderpark)

Proeflokaal Kef

CHEESE €€

7 🗺 MAP P166, C3

Specialising in Dutch and French cheese since 1953, Fromagerie Kef has a few shops around town, and here, at their canal-side tasting room/cafe, you can sample the goods. Book ahead for cheese tastings (€25 per person) or opt for a sandwich filled with Dutch aged sheep's cheese with fig compote or a cheese platter, paired with a craft beer from **Walhalla** (www.walhallacraftbeer.nl; Spijkerkade 10; ⏱4-11pm Fri, 2-11pm Sat, 2-8pm Sun; 🚊IJplein, Ⓜ️Noorderpark), a local brewery. (📞020-737 08 17; www.abrahamkef.nl; Van der Pekplein 1b; platters from €12; ⏱noon-7pm Wed, Thu & Sun, to 9pm Fri & Sat; 🚊Buiksloterweg)

Cafe Modern

GASTRONOMY €€

8 🗺 MAP P166, C3

Amid artful yet simple decor with a subtle designer feel, Cafe Modern is serious about its gastronomy yet without any stuffiness. There's a choice of a two- or three-course set lunch and a five-course set dinner, incorporating fresh seasonal ingredients on the 'surprise' menu. (📞020-494 06 84; www.modern amsterdam.nl; Meidoornweg 2; lunch 2-/3-course menu €19.50/25, dinner 5-course menu €48; ⏱noon-3pm & 6-10pm Mon-Sat; 🚊Buiksloterweg)

Cafe-Restaurant Stork

SEAFOOD €€

9 🗺 MAP P166, D4

A sometime factory on the IJ River, this huge place has a dramatically soaring interior and a cool waterfront terrace shaded with sails. It feels right that Stork should specialise in fish and seafood (though there are a few veggie and meat dishes too), serving especially good crab legs as well as other crustaceans and fish of the day. (📞020-634 40 00; www.restaurantstork.nl; Gedempt Hamerkanaal 201; mains €13-27; ⏱11am-midnight, closed Mon Oct-Mar; 🚊IJplein, Ⓜ️Noorderpark)

Pllek: Drinks in a Shipping Container

Uber-cool **Pllek** (Map p166, B1; www.pllek.nl; TT Neveritaweg 59; ⏱9.30am-1am Sun-Thu, to 3am Fri & Sat; 🚊NDSM-werf) is a Noord magnet, with hip things of all ages streaming over to hang out in its interior made of old shipping containers and, when the weather allows, lounge on its artificial sandy beach. It's a terrific spot for a waterfront drink or meal.

Drinking

Café de Ceuvel

CAFE

10 MAP P166, C2

Tucked in a former shipyard and designed by architect Wouter Valkenier, built from recycled materials and with a focus on sustainability, this waterside spot is built out onto an island. With drinks including homemade lemongrass and ginger soda, plus bottled beer from local heroes Oedipus Brewery and Brouwerij 't IJ (p162), it's a surprising oasis alongside the canal. (020-229 62 10; www.deceuvel.nl; Korte Papaverweg 4; 11am-midnight Tue-Thu & Sun, to 2am Fri & Sat; 34/35 Mosplein, Noorderpark)

Coffee Virus A-Lab

COFFEE

11 MAP P166, C4

Sharing a co-working start-up space called A-Lab with the University of Arts, this cool cafe made from mostly recycled materials is a convenient coffee stop next to A'DAM Tower. Coffee is divided into three flavour profiles – sweet, sour and bitter – and beans are sourced from local roasters. Pastries, banana bread, sandwiches, soups and salads are also on offer. (020-244 23 41; www.thecoffeevirus.nl; Overhoeksplein 2; 9am-4.30pm Mon-Fri; Buiksloterweg)

Garage Noord

BAR

12 MAP P166, E3

With its industrial setting, this small, laid-back venue has a rough-around-the-edges feel, very much in keeping with its neighbours on the up-and-coming Gedempt Hamerkanaal. Around midnight the space transforms from a casual cafe, restaurant and bar into a club playing host to a changing line-up of DJs. (06 4210 8720; www.facebook.com/garagenrd; Gedempt Hamerkanaal 40; 6pm-5am Thu-Sat; Noorderpark)

Oedipus Brewery & Tap Room

BREWERY

13 MAP P166, E4

Oedipus began with four friends trying out some experimental brewing methods, and its brightly labelled bottles are now an Amsterdam institution. This converted warehouse space is a key Noord hangout, with outdoor seating lit by coloured fairy lights. Immerse yourself in some Oedipus history by sampling Mannenliefde ('Men Love'), its first-ever beer, flavoured with lemongrass, Szechuan pepper and Sorachi Ace hops. (www.oedipus.com; Gedempt Hamerkanaal 85; 5-10pm Thu, 2-11pm Fri & Sat, 2-10pm Sun; IJplein, Noorderpark)

Entertainment

Tolhuistuin

LIVE PERFORMANCE

14 MAP P166, C4

In what was the Shell workers' canteen for 70 years from 1941, the nifty Tolhuistuin arts centre hosts African dance troupes, spoken word, visual art and much more on its garden stage under twinkling

CLAIRE BISSELL/LONELY PLANET ©

Cheese board, Café de Ceuvel

lights. It also houses club nights and big-name gigs in the Paradiso venue. (☑020-763 06 50; www.tolhuistuin.nl; IJpromenade 2; ☺cafe 11am-late, restaurant 10am-10pm; ☗Buiksloterweg)

De Ruimte
ARTS CENTRE

15 ⭐ MAP P166, C2

This arts centre and cafe hosts a changing roster of events from jazz and poetry to experimental electronica. Friday nights usually offer live music you can put your dancin' shoes on for – Ethiopian jazz, rock 'n' roll, brass bands. The cafe serves a weekly changing menu of mostly vegan global dishes. (www.cafederuimte.nl; Distelweg 83; tickets €5-10; ☺5pm-1am Thu, 5pm-3am Fri, 4pm-1am Sun; ☗IJplein, Ⓜ️Noorderpark)

Shopping

Neef Louis Design
VINTAGE

16 🔒 MAP P166, C1

A huge warehouse full of vintage, designer and industrial furniture, this is a treasure trove of antique luggage, mid-century bookcases, retro radios, neon signs and much, much more. (www.neeflouis.nl; Papaverweg 46; ☺10am-6pm Tue-Sat; ☗NDSM-werf)

Van Dijk & Ko
VINTAGE

17 🔒 MAP P166, C1

A warehouse full of interesting antiques and vintage furniture, wardrobes, glassware, prints and more for sale. (www.vandijkenko.nl; Papaverweg 46; ☺10am-6pm Tue-Sat, noon-6pm Sun; ☗NDSM-werf)

Survival Guide

An Amsterdam canal DUTCHSCENERY/SHUTTERSTOCK ©

Before You Go

Book Your Stay

○ Book as far in advance as possible, especially for festival, summer and weekend visits.

○ There's often a minimum stay of two or three nights, especially at weekends and during major events.

○ Properties often include the 7% *toeristen belasting* (tourist tax) in quoted rates, but ask before booking. If you're paying by credit card, some hotels add a surcharge of up to 5%.

Useful Websites

Lonely Planet (lonely planet.com/ the-netherlands/ amsterdam/hotels) Recommendations.

I Amsterdam (www. iamsterdam.com) Wide range of options including short-stay apartments from the city's official website.

Hotels.nl (www.hotels. nl) For deals on larger properties.

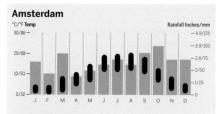

Amsterdam
°C/°F Temp — Rainfall Inches/mm

When to Go

○ **Spring** (Mar–May) Tulip time! Crowds amass around King's Day (27 April). Alternating rainy and gorgeous weather.

○ **Summer** (Jun–Aug) Peak season, warm with lots of daylight, cafe terraces boom, festivals aplenty.

○ **Autumn** (Sep–Nov) Can be rainy, off-peak rates return, the regular cultural season starts up.

○ **Winter** (Dec–Feb) Ice-skating fun, cosy cafes with fireplaces, and low-season rates ease the dark, chilly days.

○ **CityMundo** (https:// amsterdam.citymundo. com) Broker for apartment and houseboat rentals.

Best Budget

○ Cocomama (www. cocomama hostel.com) Red-curtained boutique hostel in a former brothel.

○ Generator Amsterdam (www.generator hostels. com) Designer hostel overlooking Oosterpark.

○ St Christopher's at the Winston (www. st-christophers.co.uk) Buzzing Red Light District hangout with an on-site nightclub.

○ ClinkNOORD (www. clinkhostels.com) Artsy, avant-garde hostel in Amsterdam Noord.

Best Midrange

○ SWEETS Hotel (www. sweetshotel.amsterdam) Live like Amsterdam's bridge keepers once did in one of 28 converted canal-bridge houses.

○ Hotel Fita (www.fita.nl) Sweet little family-owned hotel a stone's throw from the Museumplein.

○ Conscious Hotel Westerpark (www.conscioushotels.com) Eco innovations include recycled materials at this Westerpark hotel inside a national monument.

Best Top End

○ Hotel Okura Amsterdam (www.okura.nl) Rare-for-Amsterdam elevated views and four Michelin stars in the building.

○ Ambassade Hotel (www.ambassade-hotel.nl) Golden Age canal houses shelter this exquisite hotel with original CoBrA art on the walls.

Arriving in Amsterdam

Schiphol International Airport

Train Trains run to Amsterdam's Centraal Station (€4.50 one way, 15 minutes) 24 hours a day. From 6am to 12.30am they go every 10 minutes or so; hourly in the wee hours. The rail platform is inside the terminal, down the escalator.

Bus Connexxion Bus 397/Amsterdam Airport Express from 5.11am to 12.44am or Connexxion Bus N97 from 1.15am to 4.44am (both services €6.50 one way, 25 minutes) is the quickest way to places by Museumplein and Leidseplein. Buses depart outside the arrivals hall door. Buy a ticket from the driver (credit/debit cards only, no cash).

Taxi Taxis take 30 to 45 minutes to the centre (longer in heavy traffic), costing around €39. The taxi stand is just outside the arrivals hall door.

Lelystad Airport

Lelystad Airport (☏ 0320-284 770; www.lelystadairport.nl; Emoeweg 7), 50km east of Amsterdam, is undergoing a large expansion project (delayed in 2020 but at the time of research due to be completed in 2021) that will see it take over many budget airline and freight flights, with newly created transport links to/from Amsterdam. Check the airport website for updates.

Getting Around

Tram

○ Most public transport within the city is by tram. The vehicles are fast, frequent and ubiquitous, operating between 6am and 12.30am.

○ Tickets are sold on board by credit/debit card only (cash not accepted). Buy a disposable OV-chipkaart (www.ov-chipkaart.nl; one hour €3.20) or a day pass (one to seven days €8.50 to €36.50) from the **GVB information office** (www.gvb.nl; Stationsplein 10; ⏰7am-9pm Mon-Fri, 8am-9pm Sat, 9am-9pm Sun; ☐2/4/11/12/13/14/17/24/26 Centraal Station).

○ When you enter *and* exit, wave your card at the machine to 'check in' and 'check out'.

Metro & Bus

○ Prices for the metro and most buses are the same as trams, and use GVB's integrated ticketing system.

○ *Nachtbussen* (night buses) run after other transport stops (from 1am to 6am, every hour). A ticket costs €4.50.

○ Note that Connexxion buses (which depart from Centraal Station and are useful to reach sights in southern Amsterdam) and the No 397 airport bus are not part of the GVB system. They cost more (around €6.50).

Bicycle

○ Rental shops are everywhere.

○ You'll have to show a passport or European national ID card and leave a credit-card authorisation or pay a deposit (usually €80 to €100).

○ Prices per 24-hour period for basic 'coaster-brake' bikes average

Journey Planner

Website 9292 (www.9292.nl) calculates routes, costs and travel times, and will get you from door to door, wherever you're going in the city. The site is in English and Dutch.

€12. Bikes with gears and handbrakes cost more. Electric bikes start from €25 for 24 hours.

○ Theft insurance (from €3 per day) is strongly advised.

Ajax Bike (Map p124, C1; ☏ 06 1729 4284; www.ajaxbike.nl; Gerard Doustraat 153; bike hire per 4/24hr from €7/9.50, 3hr tours from €20; ☺10am-5.30pm Mon-Sat, noon-4pm Sun; 🚊 4 Stadhouderskade) In De Pijp.

Bike City (☏ 020-626 37 21; www.bikecity.nl; Bloemgracht 68-70; bike rental per day from €14; ☺9am-5.30pm; 🚊 13/17 Westermarkt) In the Jordaan.

Black Bikes (Map p42, B4; ☏ 0852 737 454; www.black-bikes.com; Nieuwezijds Voorburgwal 146; bike hire per 3/24hr from €6.50/9, electric bikes €24/37.50; ☺8am-8pm Mon-Fri, 9am-7pm Sat & Sun; 🚊 2/11/12/13/17 Nieuwezijds Kolk) Ten locations, including in the centre.

Damstraat Rent-a-Bike (Map p42, C6; ☏ 020-625 50 29; www.rentabike.nl; Damstraat 20-22; bike hire per 3/24hr from €7/9.50; ☺9am-6pm; 🚊 4/14/24 Dam)

Near the Dam.

MacBike (Map p42, E1; ☏ 020-624 83 91; www.macbike.nl; De Ruijterkade 34b; bike hire per 3/24hr from €7.50/9.75, electric bikes €15/25; ☺9am-6pm; 🚊 2/4/11/12/13/14/17/24/26 Centraal Station) Has a convenient location at Centraal Station, among others.

Taxi

○ Taxis are expensive and slow.

○ You don't hail taxis on the road. Instead, find them at stands at Centraal Station, Leidseplein and other busy spots around town. You needn't take the first car in the queue.

○ Another method is to book a taxi by phone. **Taxicentrale Amsterdam** (TCA; ☏ 020-777 77 77; www.tcataxi.nl) is the most reliable company.

○ Fares are meter-based. The meter starts at €3.19, then it's €2.35 per kilometre thereafter. A ride from Leidseplein to the Dam costs about €16; from Centraal Station to Jordaan is €13 to €19.

○ Ride-share service Uber (www.uber.com) operates in Amsterdam;

Tickets & Passes

o Travel passes are extremely handy and provide substantial savings over per-ride ticket purchases.

o The GVB offers unlimited-ride passes for one to seven days (€8.50 to €36.50), valid on trams, some buses and the metro.

o Passes are available at the **GVB information office** (www.gvb.nl; Stations-plein 10; ⊙7am-9pm Mon-Fri, 8am-9pm Sat, 9am-9pm Sun; 🚊2/4/11/12/13/ 14/17/24/26 Centraal Station) and **I Amsterdam Visitor Centres** (Map p42; ✆020-702 60 00; www.iamsterdam.com; Stationsplein 10; ⊙9am-6pm; 🚊2/4/11/12/13/ 14/17/24/26 Centraal Station), but not on board.

o The I Amsterdam Card (www.iamsterdam.com; per 24/48/72/96/120 hours €60/80/95/105/115) includes a GVB travel pass in its fee.

o A wider-ranging option is the Amsterdam & Region Day Ticket (€19.50), which goes beyond the tram/metro system, adding on night buses, airport buses, Connexxion buses and regional EBS buses that go to towns such as Haarlem, Muiden and Zaanse Schans. The pass is available at the GVB office and at visitor centres.

o Another choice is the Amsterdam Travel Ticket (per one/two/three days €17/22.50/28). It's basically a GVB unlimited-ride pass with an airport train ticket added on. Buy it at the airport (at the NS ticket window) or GVB office.

rates vary according to demand.

Car

o Parking is expensive and scarce.

o Street parking in the centre costs around €7.50/55 per hour/day. Pay online at www. 3377.nl.

o It's better (and cheaper) to leave your vehicle in a park-and-ride lot at the edge of town. See www.iamsterdam.com for details.

o All the big multi-national rental companies are in town; many have offices on Overtoom, near the Vondelpark.

Train

o Trains run by NS (www. ns.nl) serve the outer suburbs and, aside from travelling to/from the airport, most visitors will rarely need to use them unless undertaking trips further afield.

o Tickets can be bought at the NS service desk

windows or at ticketing machines. The ticket windows are easiest to use, though there is often a queue.

o Pay with cash, debit or credit card. Visa and MasterCard are accepted, though there is a €0.50 surcharge to use them, and they must have chip-and-PIN technology.

o There is a €1 surcharge for buying a single-use disposable ticket.

o Visitors can get a non-personalised recharge-

able OV-Chipkaart at NS windows or at GVB public transport offices. It costs €7.50 (non-refundable) and has a €20 minimum balance.

○ You must top up OV-chipkaarts at NS machines to use NS trains.

○ If you want to use a ticketing machine and pay cash, bear in mind that they accept coins only (no paper bills). The machines have instructions in English.

○ Check both in *and* out with your ticket/card. Tap it against the card reader in the gates or free-standing posts.

Essential Information

Accessible Travel

○ Travellers with reduced mobility will find Amsterdam moderately equipped to meet their needs.

○ Most offices and museums have lifts and/or ramps and toilets for visitors with disabilities.

○ A large number of budget and midrange

hotels have limited accessibility, as they occupy old buildings with steep stairs and no lifts.

○ Restaurants tend to be on ground floors, though 'ground' sometimes includes a few steps.

○ Most buses are wheelchair accessible, as are metro stations. Trams are becoming more accessible as new equipment is added. Many lines have elevated stops for wheelchair users. The GVB website (www.gvb.nl) denotes which stops are wheelchair accessible.

○ Accessible Travel Netherlands publishes a downloadable guide (www.accessibletravelnl.com) to restaurants, sights, transport and routes in Amsterdam for those with limited mobility.

○ Check the accessibility guide at Accessible Amsterdam (www.toegankelijkamsterdam.nl).

○ Download Lonely Planet's free Accessible Travel guides from https://shop.lonelyplanet.com/categories/accessible-travel.com

Business Hours

Opening hours sometimes decrease during off-peak months (October to Easter).

Cafés (pubs), bars & coffeeshops Open noon (exact hours vary); most close 1am Sunday to Thursday, 3am Friday and Saturday

General office hours 8.30am to 5pm Monday to Friday

Museums 10am to 5pm, though some close Monday

Restaurants 11am to 2.30pm and 6 to 10pm

Shops 9am/10am to 6pm Monday to Saturday, noon to 6pm Sunday. Smaller shops may keep shorter hours and/or close Monday. Many shops stay open late (to 9pm) Thursday.

Supermarkets 8am to 8pm; in the city centre some stay open until 9pm or 10pm

Discount Cards

I Amsterdam Card

(www.iamsterdam.com; per 24/48/72/96/120 hours €60/80/95/105/115) Provides admission to more than 30 museums, a canal cruise, and discounts at shops,

entertainment venues and restaurants. Also includes a GVB transit pass. Available at VVV I Amsterdam Visitor Centres.

Museumkaart (www. museumkaart.nl; adult/child €64.90/32.45, plus one-time registration €5) Free and discounted entry to some 400 museums all over the country for one year. Purchase it at participating museum ticket counters. You initially receive a temporary card valid for 31 days (maximum five museums); you can then register it online and receive a permanent card sent to a Dutch address, such as your hotel, within three to five working days.

Holland Pass (www. hollandpass.com; three/four/six attractions from €45/60/75) Similar to the I Amsterdam Card, but without the rush for usage; you can visit sights over a month. Prices are based on the number of attractions, which you pick from tiers (the most popular/expensive sights are gold tier). Also includes a train ticket from the airport to the city, and a canal cruise. Purchase it online; pick-up locations include Schiphol Airport and the city centre.

Electricity

Type C
230V/50Hz

Type F
230V/50Hz

Money

ATMs

ATMs can be found outside most banks, at the airport and at Centraal Station. Most accept credit cards such as Visa and MasterCard, as well as cash cards that access the Cirrus and Plus networks. Check with your home bank for service charges before leaving.

In the city centre and at the airport, ATMs often have queues or run out of cash on weekends.

Cash

A surprising number of businesses do not accept credit cards, so it's wise to have cash on hand. (Conversely, many places only accept cards.)

Changing Money

Use GWK Travelex (www.gwk.nl), which has several branches around town:

GWK Travelex Centraal Station
(☎ 020-627 27 31; www. gwktravelex.nl; Stationsplein 13f; ⏱10am-5pm; 🚊2/4/11/12/13/14/17/24/26 Centraal Station)

GWK Travelex Leidseplein (☎ 020-622 14 25; www.gwktravelex.nl; Leidsestraat 103; ⏰ 9am-9pm Mon-Fri, from 10am Sat, 10am-8pm Sun; 🚊 1/2/5/7/11/12/19 Leidseplein)

GWK Travelex Schiphol Airport (☎ 020-653 51 21; www.gwktravelex.nl; Arrival Hall 3; ⏰ 6am-10pm)

Credit Cards

All the major international credit cards are recognised, and most hotels and large stores accept them. But a fair number of shops, restaurants and other businesses, such as some supermarkets, do not accept credit cards, or only accept debit cards with chip-and-PIN technology. Be aware that foreign-issued cards (even chip-and-PIN-enabled foreign credit or debit cards) aren't always accepted (including in some ticket machines), so check first.

Some establishments levy a 5% surcharge (or more) on credit cards to offset the commissions charged by card providers. Always ask beforehand.

Currency

The Netherlands uses the euro (€). Unlike many eurozone countries, one- and two-cent coins aren't used in the Netherlands.

Tipping

Bars Not expected.

Hotels Tip €1 to €2 per bag for porters; cleaning staff get a few euros for a job well done.

Restaurants Leave 5% to 10% for a cafe snack (if your bill comes to €9.50, you might round up to €10), 10% or so for a restaurant meal.

Taxis Tip 5% to 10%, or round up to the nearest euro.

Public Holidays

Most museums adopt Sunday hours on public holidays (except Christmas and New Year, when they close), even if they fall on a day when the place would otherwise be closed, such as Monday.

Nieuwjaarsdag (New Year's Day) 1 January

Goede Vrijdag (Good Friday) March/April

Eerste Paasdag (Easter Sunday) March/April

Tweede Paasdag (Easter Monday) March/April

Koningsdag (King's Day) 27 April (26 April if 27 April is a Sunday)

Dodenherdenking (Remembrance Day) 4 May (unofficial)

Bevrijdingsdag (Liberation Day) 5 May (unofficially celebrated annually; officially every five years, next in 2025)

Hemelvaartsdag (Ascension Day) 40th day after Easter Sunday

Eerste Pinksterdag (Whit Sunday; Pentecost) 50th day after Easter Sunday

Tweede Pinksterdag (Whit Monday) 50th day after Easter Monday

Eerste Kerstdag (Christmas Day) 25 December

Tweede Kerstdag (Second Christmas; Boxing Day) 26 December

Safe Travel

Amsterdam is a safe and manageable city and if you use your common sense you should have no problems.

○ Stay alert for pickpockets in tourist-heavy zones such as Centraal

Station, the Bloemen-markt and the Red Light District.

○ Avoid deserted streets in the Red Light District at night.

○ It is forbidden to take photos of women in the Red Light District windows; this is strictly enforced.

○ Be careful around the canals. Almost none of them have fences or barriers.

○ Watch out for bicycles; never walk in bicycle lanes and always look carefully before you cross one.

○ Covid-19 travel restrictions and requirements for visiting the Netherlands are updated in English at www.government.nl. For details of current measures in Amsterdam during your visit check www.amsterdam.nl/en/coronavirus/covid19.

Toilets

○ Public toilets are not a widespread facility on Dutch streets, apart from the free-standing public urinals for men in places such as the Red Light District.

○ Many people duck into a *café* (pub; ask first!) or department store.

○ The standard fee for toilet attendants is €0.50.

○ The app HogeNood (High Need; www.hogenood.nu) maps the nearest toilets based on your location.

Tourist Information

I Amsterdam Visitor Centre (Map p42, E2; ☎ 020-702 60 00; www.iamsterdam.com; Stationsplein 10; ⊙ 9am-6pm; 🚊 2/4/11/12/13/14/17/24/26 Centraal Station) Main branch; located in front of Centraal Station. Sells discount cards, theatre and museum tickets, maps and public-transit passes.

I Amsterdam Store (Map p42, E1; www.iamsterdam.com; De Ruijterkade 28a, Centraal Station; ⊙ 8am-7pm Mon-Wed, to 8pm Thu-Sat, 10am-6pm Sun; 🚊 2/4/11/12/13/14/17/24/26 Centraal Station) Situated behind Centraal Station on De Ruijterkade, this official Amsterdam store sells tickets to events, tourist passes and Dutch products.

I Amsterdam Visitor Centre Schiphol (www.iamsterdam.com; Arrival Hall 2; ⊙ 7am-10pm) Inside Schiphol International Airport, this office provides maps, and sells discount cards and tickets to major attractions.

Visas

○ Citizens of the US, Canada, Australia, New Zealand and the UK currently need only a valid passport to enter nearly all countries in Europe, including the entire EU. However, in late 2022, the EU will introduce a new visa-waiver scheme called ETIAS (European Travel Information and Authorization System). Citizens of visa-exempt countries will subsequently have to fill in an online application and pay €7. The authorization will be valid for three years.

○ The Netherlands is part of the Schengen agreement, which includes all EU states (minus Britain and Ireland) and a handful of European countries including Switzerland. In general, a visa issued by one Schengen country is good for all of the other

Dos & Don'ts

Greetings Do give a firm handshake and a double or triple cheek kiss.

Marijuana & alcohol Don't smoke dope or drink beer on the streets.

Smoking Don't smoke (any substance) in bars or restaurants.

Bluntness Don't take offence if locals give you a frank, unvarnished opinion. It's not considered impolite, rather it comes from the desire to be direct and honest.

Cycling paths Don't walk in bike lanes (which are marked by white lines and bicycle symbols), and do look both ways before crossing one.

member countries.

o Because regulations can change, double-check with your embassy or consulate before travelling.

o The Netherlands Foreign Affairs Ministry (www.government. nl) lists consulates and embassies around the world. Visas and extensions are handled by the Immigratie en Naturalisatie dienst (Immigration & Naturalisation Service; www.ind. nl). Study visas must be applied for via your college or university in the Netherlands.

Responsible Travel

The municipality's plan to counteract over-tourism, *Stad in Balans* (City in Balance; www. amsterdam.nl/en/policy/policy-city-balance), aims to make the city more liveable for residents and welcoming for travellers. Measures being considered include banning foreign residents from coffeeshops (cannabis cafes),

relocating brothels from the Red Light District to a purpose-built centre outside the city, addressing private accommodation rentals in the city centre (an outright ban was overturned in court at the timing of writing) and limiting overnight tourist stays to between 10 and 20 million per year.

Top Tips

o Skip busy weekends and visit mid-week if possible.

o Reduce your environmental footprint: travel by train rather than flying; walk, cycle or rent an electric boat; look for companies that make a positive impact, such as Instock (www.instock. nl), which minimises food waste.

o Check with your provider to ensure your holiday rental accommodation has a permit.

o Explore neighbourhoods outside the centre and areas further afield.

o Shop for locally made items such as Dutch design.

Language

The pronunciation of Dutch is fairly straightforward. If you read our coloured pronunciation guides as if they were English, you'll be understood just fine. Note that **öy** is pronounced as the 'er y' (without the 'r') in 'her year', and kh is a throaty sound, similar to the 'ch' in the Scottish *loch*. The stressed syllables are indicated with italics.

Where relevant, both polite and informal options in Dutch are included, indicated with 'pol' and 'inf' respectively.

To enhance your trip with a phrasebook, visit lonelyplanet. com. Lonely Planet iPhone phrasebooks are available through the Apple App store.

Basics

Hello.	*Dag./Hallo.*	dakh/ha·loh
Goodbye.	*Dag.*	dakh
Yes.	*Ja.*	yaa
No.	*Nee.*	ney

Please.
Alstublieft. (pol) al·stew·*bleeft*
Alsjeblieft. (inf) a·shuh·*bleeft*

Thank you.
Dank u/je. (pol/inf) dangk ew/yuh

Excuse me.
Excuseer mij. eks·kew·*zeyr* mey

How are you?
Hoe gaat het met hoo khaat huht met
u/jou? (pol/inf) ew/yaw

Fine. And you?
Goed. En met khoot en met
u/jou? (pol/inf) ew/yaw

Do you speak English?
Spreekt u Engels? spreykt ew *eng*·uhls

I don't understand.
Ik begrijp ik buh·*khreyp*
het niet. huht neet

Eating & Drinking

I'd like ...
Ik wil graag ... ik wil khraakh ...

a beer	*een bier*	uhn beer
a coffee	*een koffie*	uhn *ko*·fee
a table for two	*een tafel voor twee*	uhn *taa*·fuhl vohr twey
the menu	*een menu*	uhn me·*new*

I don't eat (meat).
Ik eet geen (vlees). ik eyt kheyn (vleys)

Delicious!
Heerlijk!/Lekker! heyr·luhk/le·kuhr

Cheers!
Proost! prohst

Please bring the bill.
Mag ik de makh ik duh
rekening rey·kuh·ning
alstublieft? al·stew·*bleeft*

Shopping

I'd like to buy ...
Ik wil graag ... ik wil khraakh ...
kopen. koh·puhn

I'm just looking.
Ik kijk alleen maar. ik keyk a·*leyn* maar

How much is it?
Hoeveel kost het?   hoo·*veyl* kost huht

That's too expensive.
Dat is te duur.   dat is tuh dewr

Can you lower the price?
Kunt u wat van   kunt ew wat van
de prijs afdoen?   duh preys *af*·doon

Emergencies

Help!
Help!   help

Call a doctor!
Bel een dokter!   bel uhn *dok*·tuhr

Call the police!
Bel de politie!   bel duh poh·*leet*·see

I'm sick.
Ik ben ziek.   ik ben zeek

I'm lost.
Ik ben verdwaald.   ik ben vuhr·*dwaalt*

Where are the toilets?
Waar zijn de   waar zeyn duh
toiletten?   twa·*le*·tuhn

Time & Numbers

What time is it?
Hoe laat is het?   hoo laat is huht

It's (10) o'clock.
Het is (tien) uur.   huht is (teen) ewr

Half past (10).
Half (elf).   half (elf)
(lit: half eleven)

morning	*'s ochtends*	*sokh*·tuhns
afternoon	*'s middags*	*smi*·dakhs
evening	*'s avonds*	*saa*·vonts

yesterday	*gisteren*	*khis*·tuh·ruhn
today	*vandaag*	van·*daakh*
tomorrow	*morgen*	*mor*·khuhn

1	*één*	eyn
2	*twee*	twey
3	*drie*	dree
4	*vier*	veer
5	*vijf*	veyf
6	*zes*	zes
7	*zeven*	*zey*·vuhn
8	*acht*	akht
9	*negen*	*ney*·khuhn
10	*tien*	teen

Transport & Directions

Where's the ...?
Waar is ...?   waar is ...

How far is it?
Hoe ver is het?   hoo ver is huht

What's the address?
Wat is het adres?   wat is huht a·*dres*

Can you show me (on the map)?
Kunt u het mij   kunt ew huht mey
tonen (op de   *toh*·nuhn (op duh
kaart)?   kaart)

A ticket to ..., please.
Een kaartje naar   uhn *kaar*·chuh naar
..., graag.   ... khraakh

Please take me to ...
Breng me   breng muh
alstublieft   al·*stew*·bleeft
naar ...   naar ...

Does it stop at ...?
Stopt het in ...?   stopt huht in ...

I'd like to get off at ...
Ik wil graag in ...   ik wil khraak in ...
uitstappen.   *öyt*·sta·puhn

Can we get there by bike?
Kunnen we er   *ku*·nuhn wuh uhr
met de fiets heen?   met duh feets heyn

Behind the Scenes

Send Us Your Feedback

We love to hear from travellers – your comments help make our books better. We read every word, and we guarantee that your feedback goes straight to the authors. Visit **lonelyplanet.com/contact** to submit your updates and suggestions.

Note: We may edit, reproduce and incorporate your comments in Lonely Planet products such as guidebooks, websites and digital products, so let us know if you don't want your comments reproduced or your name acknowledged. For a copy of our privacy policy visit lonelyplanet.com/privacy.

Catherine's Thanks

Hartelijk bedankt first and foremost to Julian, and to everyone in Amsterdam and throughout the Netherlands, who provided insights, inspiration and good times during this update and over the years. Huge thanks, too, to my Amsterdam co-authors Kate and Barbara, and to everyone at LP. As ever, *merci encore* to my parents, brother, *belle-sœur*, *neveu* and *nièce*.

Kate's Thanks

A big thank you to Lonely Planet for commissioning me to work on this fantastic city. Thank you to Christa Doorhof and all of the staff at I Amsterdam for your assistance, and to the many people in Amsterdam who provided assistance and gave me local tips along the way. Finally, a huge thanks to my partner Trent for travelling with me and for all of your support.

Barbara's Thanks

A big heartfelt thanks to all those who have helped in my career along the way, leading to this dream of completing my first Lonely Planet project (in no particular order): Clair Woolsey, Remy Woolsey, René Frank, Marlene Dow and family, Debby Harris, Dixie Michie, Brenda Woolsey-Hartford, Bhec Fernandez, Alyssa Gabrielle and Allexa Scarlet Masongsong, Nolan Janssen, Marc Linneweber, Alexa Kaminsky, Garth and Gloria Pickard, Andrea Schulte-Peevers, and Nicola Williams.

Acknowledgements

Cover photograph: Dutch houses, boat and canal in the center of Amsterdam, Aleksandar Georgiev/ Getty Images ©

Photographs pp30-1 (clockwise from top left): Anibal Trejo/ Shutterstock ©, DutchScenery/ Shutterstock ©, Dennis van de Water/Shutterstock ©

This Book

This 7th edition of Lonely Planet's *Pocket Amsterdam* guidebook was researched and written by Catherine Le Nevez, Kate Morgan and Barbara Woolsey. This guidebook was produced by the following:

Destination Editors
Matt Phillips, Daniel Fahey

Senior Product Editors Sandie Kestell, Genna Patterson

Regional Senior Cartographer
Mark Griffiths

Product Editors Will Allen, Hannah Cartmel

Cartographer Julie Dodkins

Book Designers
Aomi Ito, Norma Prause-Brewer

Assisting Editors
James Bainbridge, Michelle Bennett, Lorna Parkes, Tamara Sheward, Simon Williamson

Assisting Book Designer
Jessica Rose

Cover Researcher
Brendan Dempsey-Spencer

Thanks to Katie Connolly, Myfanwy Ferris, Sonia Kapoor, Kate Kiely, Andrew Watson

Index

See also separate subindexes for:

⊗ **Eating p189**

⊙ **Drinking p190**

☆ **Entertainment p190**

🔒 **Shopping p191**

Our Writers

Catherine Le Nevez

Catherine's wanderlust kicked in when she roadtripped across Europe from her Parisian base aged four, and she's been hitting the road at every opportunity since, travelling to some 60 countries and completing her Doctorate of Creative Arts in Writing, Masters in Professional Writing, and postgrad qualifications in Editing and Publishing along the way. Over the past decade and a half she's written scores of Lonely Planet guides.

Kate Morgan

Having worked for Lonely Planet for over a decade, Kate has been fortunate enough to cover plenty of ground working as a travel writer on destinations such as Shanghai, Japan, India, Russia, Zimbabwe, the Philippines and Phuket. She has had stints living in London, Paris and Osaka but these days is based in one of her favourite regions in the world – Victoria, Australia.

Barbara Woolsey

Barbara was born and raised on the Canadian prairies to a Filipino mother and Irish-Scottish father – and that third-culture-kid upbringing has fuelled a life's passion for cross-cultural storytelling. Barbara's career started in Bangkok working for Thailand's largest English-language newspaper, then travelling around Asia as a TV host for a Bangkok-based channel. Since then, she's voyaged across over 40 countries and five continents.

Published by Lonely Planet Global Limited
CRN 554153
7th edition – Feb 2022
ISBN 978 1 78868 852 9
© Lonely Planet 2022   Photographs © as indicated 2022
10 9 8 7 6 5 4 3 2 1
Printed in Malaysia